FAVORITE ALL TIME RECIPES™

PIZZA
LOVERS'
COLLECTION

PUBLICATIONS INTERNATIONAL, LTD.

Front cover photography by Sacco Productions Limited, Chicago.

Pictured on the front cover: Homemade Pizza (page 74).

8 7 6 5 4 3 2 1

Manufactured in U.S.A.

Microwave ovens vary in wattage. The microwave cooking times in this
publication are approximate. Use the cooking times as guidelines and
check for doneness before adding more time. Consult manufacturer's
instructions for suitable microwave-safe cooking dishes.

PIZZA LOVERS'

COLLECTION

PARTY PIZZETTES

Good food and great parties go hand in hand. So why not start your next bash with a pizza appetizer? Choose from a variety of mini pizza pizzettes such as Individual Party Pizzas and Cheesy Crab Squares.

PIZZA VIA VENETO

Makes about 3 dozen appetizers

1 box (16 ounces) hot roll mix
2 eggs
½ cup evaporated milk
⅓ cup peanut butter
¼ cup chopped pimiento
1 teaspoon celery seed
4 cups shredded Cheddar cheese
3 cups chopped salted peanuts
¼ teaspoon pepper

Prepare hot roll mix and let rise as package directs. Divide dough into two equal parts. Pat each part, using oiled hands, into well-oiled 15×10×1-inch jelly-roll pan. Beat eggs, milk and peanut butter until smooth. Add pimiento and celery seed. Stir in cheese; spread evenly over dough, almost to edge. Sprinkle with peanuts and pepper. Cover; let rise 30 minutes.

Preheat oven to 425°F. Bake 12 to 15 minutes or until brown and bubbly. Cut into 4×2-inch rectangles. Serve hot.

Favorite recipe from **Oklahoma Peanut Commission**

MOLLETES
(Mexican Toasts)

Makes 16 to 20 appetizers

IMPERIAL® Margarine
8 to 10 French rolls, cut lengthwise into halves or quarters
LAWRY'S® Garlic Powder with Parsley
1 can (16 ounces) refried beans
Salsa
2 cups (8 ounces) grated Cheddar or Monterey Jack cheese

Spread margarine on rolls; lightly sprinkle on Garlic Powder with Parsley. Toast under broiler until just golden. Spread each with refried beans and salsa. Top with cheese. Place under broiler to melt cheese.

Presentation: Serve with guacamole.

Molletes (Mexican Toasts)

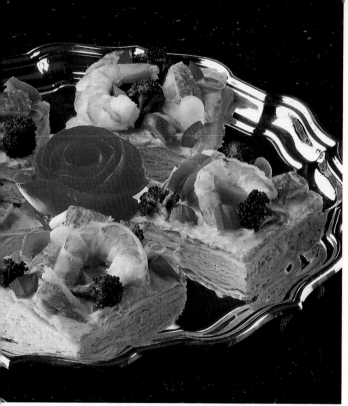

Seafood Pizza Primavera

SEAFOOD PIZZA PRIMAVERA

Makes one 15×10-inch pie

2 (8-ounce) packages refrigerated
  crescent rolls
1 (8-ounce) container BORDEN®
  or MEADOW GOLD® Sour
  Cream
½ cup BENNETT'S® Chili, Cocktail
  or Hot Seafood Sauce
¼ pound peeled, cooked small
  shrimp *or* 1 (4¼-ounce) can
  ORLEANS® Shrimp, drained
  and soaked as label directs
¼ pound imitation crab blend,
  flaked *or* 1 (6-ounce) can
  HARRIS® or ORLEANS® Crab
  Meat, drained
1 cup chopped broccoli
½ cup sliced green onions
½ cup chopped green bell pepper
½ cup chopped red bell pepper

Preheat oven to 400°F. Unroll
crescent roll dough; press on bottom
of 15×10-inch baking sheet,
pressing perforations together. Bake
10 minutes or until golden. Cool.
Combine sour cream and sauce;
spread over crust. Top with
remaining ingredients. Chill. Cut
into squares to serve. Refrigerate
leftovers.

VEGETABLE PIZZA

Makes about 24 appetizers

1 can (8 ounces) refrigerated
  crescent dinner rolls
1 package (8 ounces)
  PHILADELPHIA BRAND®
  Cream Cheese, softened
½ cup MIRACLE WHIP® or
  MIRACLE WHIP LIGHT®
  Dressing
½ teaspoon Italian seasoning
¾ cup chopped red pepper
¾ cup chopped radishes
½ cup sliced pitted ripe olives
2 tablespoons sliced green onions
½ cup (2 ounces) KRAFT® Natural
  Shredded Sharp Cheddar
  Cheese

• Heat oven to 375°F.

• Unroll dough into 2 rectangles.
Press onto bottom and ¼-inch up
sides of 13×9-inch baking pan to
form crust.

• Bake 10 minutes; cool.

• Mix cream cheese, dressing and
seasoning until well blended. Spread
over crust. Top with remaining
ingredients. Refrigerate. Cut into
squares.

Prep time: 20 minutes plus
refrigerating

TORTILLA PIZZAS

Makes 4 appetizer pizzas

2 tablespoons butter or margarine
2 cups chopped cooked chicken
1 teaspoon dried oregano leaves, crushed
½ teaspoon salt
⅛ teaspoon ground black pepper
    Vegetable oil
4 (6-inch) corn tortillas
8 tablespoons chopped tomato
8 tablespoons thinly sliced green onions
4 tablespoons chopped green pepper
8 tablespoons pizza sauce
1 cup (4 ounces) shredded Cheddar or mozzarella cheese
    Chili peppers (optional)

Preheat oven to 375°F. Melt butter in medium skillet over medium heat. Add chicken, oregano, salt and black pepper; cook and stir 3 to 5 minutes. Remove chicken from skillet with slotted spoon; place in bowl and reserve.

Pour oil into same skillet to ¼ inch depth; heat oil over medium-high heat. Cook 1 tortilla in hot oil about 1 minute or until crisp. Remove tortilla from skillet; drain on paper towels and place on large baking sheet. Repeat with remaining tortillas. Spoon ¼ of chicken mixture evenly over each tortilla. Top each with 2 tablespoons tomato, 2 tablespoons onion, 1 tablespoon green pepper, 2 tablespoons pizza sauce and ¼ cup cheese. Bake 5 minutes or until cheese melts. Garnish with chili peppers, if desired.

QUESADILLA PIZZA

Makes 2 appetizer servings

2 flour tortillas (6 to 7 inches)
¼ cup shredded Cheddar cheese
    Olive oil
¼ cup CONTADINA® Pizza Squeeze Pizza Sauce
¼ teaspoon ground cumin
2 tablespoons refried beans
1 tablespoon diced green chiles
1 tablespoon thinly sliced green onion
1 tablespoon sliced ripe olives
1 tablespoon shredded Monterey Jack cheese

Sprinkle one tortilla with Cheddar cheese; top with second tortilla. Brush lightly with oil; place on baking sheet. Bake in preheated 450°F. oven for 4 minutes. In small bowl, combine pizza sauce and cumin; spread on tortilla. Spoon on refried beans; sprinkle with chiles, green onion, olives and Monterey Jack cheese. Bake in preheated 450°F. oven for 3 minutes longer or until cheese is melted. Cut into wedges.

Tortilla Pizza

INDIVIDUAL PARTY PIZZAS

Makes 6 appetizer servings

**Pizza Crust Dough
   (recipe follows)**
8 ounces fresh Italian sausage
1 tablespoon olive oil
1 medium onion, chopped
1 clove garlic, minced
**1 can (16 ounces) plum or whole
   tomatoes, broken up**
**1 teaspoon dried basil leaves,
   crushed**
**1 teaspoon dried oregano leaves,
   crushed**
½ teaspoon salt
**½ teaspoon dried rosemary leaves,
   crushed**
4 ounces pepperoni, thinly sliced
**1 small green or red bell pepper,
   cut into ½-inch pieces**
1 small onion, coarsely chopped
¼ pound fresh mushrooms, sliced
**1 can (2¼ ounces) sliced ripe
   olives, drained**
**1 jar (6 ounces) marinated,
   quartered artichoke hearts,
   drained and halved
   Crushed dried red pepper**
**3 cups (12 ounces) shredded
   mozzarella cheese**
**¼ cup (1 ounce) grated Parmesan
   cheese**

Prepare Pizza Crust Dough. Remove and discard casing from sausage. Heat small skillet over medium heat until hot. Crumble sausage into skillet. Cook, stirring to separate meat, until no pink remains. Pour off drippings; set aside.

Heat oil in medium skillet over medium-high heat. Add medium onion and garlic; cook and stir until onion is soft. Add tomatoes, basil, oregano, salt and rosemary. Reduce heat to low; simmer, uncovered, 30 minutes, stirring occasionally. Cool.

Preheat oven to 425°F. Spread an equal amount of sauce over each prebaked crust. Divide sausage and ½ of pepperoni over crusts. Place green pepper, small onion, mushrooms, olives, artichoke hearts and crushed red pepper evenly over crusts as desired. Top with remaining pepperoni and cheeses. Place pizzas on baking sheets; bake 12 to 14 minutes or until heated through.

Pizza Crust Dough

2½ to 3 cups flour, divided
**1 package (¼ ounce) fast-rising
   dry yeast**
1 teaspoon sugar
½ teaspoon salt
**1 cup warm water
   (105° to 115°F)**
**2 tablespoons olive oil
   Cornmeal**

Combine 2½ cups flour, yeast, sugar and salt in large bowl. Add water and oil; beat with electric mixer at low speed 1 minute. Beat at high speed 3 minutes. Stir in enough of remaining ½ cup flour to form soft dough. Turn out onto lightly floured surface. Knead 8 to 10 minutes or until dough is elastic. Place in lightly greased bowl; turn to coat. Cover; let rise in warm place until double in bulk, about 45 minutes. Punch down dough; divide into six pieces. Cover; let rest 10 minutes. Roll each piece of dough into a 7-inch circle; prick several times with fork. Cover; let rest 10 minutes.

Preheat oven to 425°F. Generously grease two baking sheets; sprinkle with cornmeal. Place pizzas on baking sheet; bake 8 to 9 minutes or until golden brown. Cool on wire racks.   *Makes 6 (7-inch) crusts*

Favorite recipe from **National Live Stock and Meat Board**

Individual Party Pizzas

CHAVRIE® & BASIL PIZZA BITES

Makes 12 slices

**1 (5.3-ounce) container
   CHAVRIE® goat cheese**
2 cloves garlic, minced
**½ teaspoon dried oregano leaves,
   crushed**
¼ teaspoon fresh ground pepper
1 small loaf French bread
**2 plum tomatoes, thinly sliced
   Olive oil**
½ cup shredded fresh basil leaves

Preheat oven to 400°F.

Combine Chavrie®, garlic, oregano
and pepper. Mix well. Cut French
bread into 12 slices. Top each slice
with slice of tomato and brush with
olive oil. Place 1 teaspoon of cheese
mixture on top of each tomato slice;
bake 8 to 10 minutes or until bread
is toasted. Remove from oven and
top with shredded basil.

Favorite recipe from **Bongrain Cheese U.S.A.**

KONA COAST PIZZA

Makes 2 appetizer servings

**2 tablespoons CONTADINA®
   Pizza Squeeze Pizza Sauce**
¼ teaspoon hoisin sauce
1 English muffin, split and toasted
**1 tablespoon coarsely chopped
   water chestnuts**
**1 tablespoon chopped red bell
   pepper**
**2 tablespoons drained, crushed
   pineapple**
**2 tablespoons thinly sliced ham,
   cut in strips**
**1 tablespoon shredded
   mozzarella cheese**
**1 tablespoon thinly sliced green
   onion**

In small bowl, combine pizza sauce
and hoisin sauce; spread on English
muffin halves. Top with water
chestnuts, bell pepper, pineapple,
ham, cheese and green onion. Place
on baking sheet; bake in preheated
450°F. oven for 5 minutes.

CHEESY CRAB SQUARES

Makes about 24 appetizers

2 cans (8 ounces each) refrigerated crescent dinner rolls
1/2 cup MIRACLE WHIP® or MIRACLE WHIP LIGHT® Dressing
2 teaspoons lemon juice
1/8 teaspoon pepper
2 cups (8 ounces) KRAFT® Natural Shredded Sharp Cheddar Cheese
2 cups (6 ounces) imitation crabmeat, chopped
1/3 cup green onion slices
1 tablespoon chopped parsley

• Heat oven to 375°F.

• Unroll dough into 4 rectangles. Press onto bottom and halfway up sides of 15×10×1-inch baking pan to form crust.

• Bake 10 minutes.

• Mix dressing, juice and pepper. Add cheese, imitation crabmeat, onions and parsley; mix lightly.

• Spread mixture over crust. Continue baking 12 to 15 minutes or until cheese is melted. Let stand 5 minutes; cut into squares.

Prep time: 15 minutes
Cooking time: 25 minutes plus standing

To make ahead: Prepare crust as directed; cool. Cover tightly. Prepare imitation crabmeat mixture as directed; cover. Refrigerate. Spread imitation crabmeat mixture on crust just before serving. Bake at 350°F, 15 minutes or until cheese is melted.

OLIVE PIZZA BREAD

Makes 10 appetizer servings

1 package (13¾ ounces) hot roll mix*
1 can (10½ ounces) pizza sauce
2 tablespoons vegetable oil
1 clove garlic, minced
1/2 teaspoon dried oregano leaves, crushed
1/2 teaspoon dried basil leaves, crushed
1/3 cup grated Parmesan cheese
1½ cups pitted California ripe olives, sliced
1/4 cup minced parsley

Prepare hot roll mix according to package directions to form dough. Pat dough into greased 15×10×1-inch baking pan. Make deep indentations in dough at 1-inch intervals with finger. Let rise, covered, in warm place (85°F) until doubled, about 45 minutes.

Preheat oven to 450°F. Mix pizza sauce, oil, garlic, oregano and basil in small bowl. Spread 1/2 of sauce mixture on top of dough; sprinkle with cheese.

Bake 8 minutes. Sprinkle olives over partially baked dough; drizzle with remaining sauce. Sprinkle with parsley. Bake 5 minutes longer or until edges are light brown. Cut into 5×3-inch rectangles. Serve hot.

Note: Wrap bread well and freeze, if desired. To reheat, unwrap and place on baking sheet; bake in 350°F oven about 25 minutes.

1 can (10 ounces) refrigerated pizza crust may also be used; unroll and press into greased 15×10×1-inch baking pan.

Favorite recipe from **California Olive Industry**

Cheesy Crab Squares

ARIZONA CHEESE CRISP

Makes 4 to 6 appetizer servings

Vegetable oil for deep-frying
2 flour tortillas, 10 to 12 inches
in diameter
1 to 1½ cups (4 to 6 ounces)
shredded Cheddar or
Monterey Jack cheese
½ cup picante sauce
¼ cup grated Parmesan cheese

Pour oil into wok to depth of 1 inch. Place over medium-high heat until oil registers 360°F on deep-frying thermometer. (You can also test oil by standing wooden chopstick on bottom of wok; oil should bubble gently around base of chopstick.) Slide 1 tortilla into oil. Using 2 slotted spoons, gently hold center of tortilla down so oil flows over edges. When tortilla is crisp and golden on bottom, carefully tilt wok, holding tortilla in place with spoon, to cover edge of tortilla with oil; cook until lightly browned. Rotate tortilla as needed so entire edge is lightly browned. Remove from oil and drain on paper towels, curled side down. Repeat with second tortilla. Tortillas can be made up to 8 hours in advance. Cover loosely and let stand at room temperature.

Preheat oven to 350°F. Place shells, curled side up, on baking sheet. Sprinkle each with ½ of Cheddar cheese; top each with ½ of picante sauce. Sprinkle Parmesan cheese evenly over tops. Bake, uncovered, 8 to 10 minutes or until cheeses melt.

Arizona Cheese Crisp

TACOS BOTANAS (Snacks)

Makes 1 dozen appetizers

2 packages (8 ounces each)
refrigerated pizza dough
2 cups (3 medium) grated
zucchini
1 can (16 ounces) refried beans
1 package (1.25 ounces)
LAWRY'S® Taco Spices &
Seasonings
½ cup dairy sour cream
Salsa
1 cup (4 ounces) grated Cheddar
cheese
½ cup sliced green onions
1 can (2¼ ounces) sliced ripe
olives, drained

Roll dough to fit into a 15½×10½×1-inch jelly-roll pan. Bake in 425°F oven 15 minutes or until crisp around edges. Let cool. In small bowl, combine zucchini, refried beans and Taco Spices & Seasonings. Spread bean mixture and sour cream on baked crust. Drizzle on salsa; top with cheese, green onions and olives. Return to oven to melt cheese. Cut into squares. Serve immediately or cover and refrigerate.

Presentation: Serve as an appetizer or as an afternoon snack.

MEDITERRANEAN APPETIZER

Makes 8 servings

1 (8 oz.) container Light
   PHILADELPHIA BRAND®
   Pasteurized Process Cream
   Cheese Product
2 teaspoons red wine vinegar
1 garlic clove, minced
½ teaspoon dried oregano leaves,
   crushed
½ teaspoon lemon pepper
   seasoning
24 (3 inch) lahvosh crackers or
   4 pita bread rounds, split
1½ cups finely torn spinach
1 tomato, chopped
4 ozs. CHURNY ATHENOS® Feta
   Cheese, crumbled
½ cup Greek ripe olives, pitted,
   chopped

• Stir together cream cheese
product, vinegar, garlic and
seasonings in small bowl until well
blended.

• Spread crackers with cream cheese
mixture. Top with remaining
ingredients.

Prep time: 20 minutes

Variation: Substitute one 15-inch
lahvosh cracker bread for individual
crackers. Prepare according to
package directions.

Note: Lahvosh is a Middle Eastern
sesame seed crisp cracker bread.
Traditionally eaten as a cracker, it
can be softened by holding under
cold water, then placing between
two damp towels for about 1 hour.

Mediterranean Appetizer

HIDDEN VALLEY RANCH® ARTICHOKE PIZZA

Makes 36 appetizers

2 (8-ounce) cans refrigerated
   crescent dinner rolls
¼ cup prepared HIDDEN VALLEY
   RANCH® Milk Recipe
   Original Ranch® Salad
   Dressing
1 (14-ounce) can artichoke
   hearts, quartered and drained
1 (4-ounce) jar sliced pimentos,
   drained
¾ cup shredded mozzarella
   cheese
¾ cup grated Parmesan cheese,
   divided

Preheat oven to 375°F. Unroll dough
without tearing, press into
15×10×1-inch pan. Bake 10
minutes or until cooked through.
Combine remaining ingredients,
reserving ¼ cup Parmesan cheese.
Spread on crust. Bake 15 minutes
longer. Let stand 5 minutes. Sprinkle
with reserved Parmesan cheese. Cut
into 2-inch squares.

PESTO PIZZA

Makes 32 appetizers

2 loaves (2 ounces each) regular size SAHARA® Pita Bread
½ cup HELLMANN'S® or BEST FOODS® Real, Light Reduced Calorie or Reduced Fat Cholesterol Free Mayonnaise Dressing
½ cup grated Parmesan cheese
½ cup chopped fresh basil
¼ cup pine nuts, toasted
1 small clove garlic, minced or pressed
Fresh basil leaves for garnish (optional)

Preheat oven to 375°F. Cut each pita bread around edge, separating halves. Place cut-side up in shallow pan. Bake, turning once, 8 minutes or until slightly crisp. In small bowl combine mayonnaise, Parmesan, basil, pine nuts and garlic until blended. Spread evenly on pitas. Bake 8 minutes or until puffed and lightly browned. Cut each into 8 wedges. If desired, garnish with basil leaves.

Winter Pesto Pizza: Follow recipe for Pesto Pizza. Omit fresh basil. Add ½ cup chopped fresh parsley and ½ teaspoon dried basil.

MEXICAN PIZZAS

Makes 6 to 8 appetizer servings

Red & Green Salsa (recipe follows) (optional)
8 ounces chorizo sausage
1 cup (4 ounces) shredded mild Cheddar cheese
1 cup (4 ounces) shredded Monterey Jack cheese
3 flour tortillas (10-inch diameter)

Prepare Red & Green Salsa; set aside. Remove and discard casing from chorizo. Heat medium skillet over high heat until hot. Reduce heat to medium. Crumble chorizo into skillet. Cook, stirring to separate meat, until no pink remains. Remove with slotted spoon; drain on paper towels.

Preheat oven to 450°F. Combine cheeses in small bowl. Place tortillas on baking sheets. Divide chorizo evenly among tortillas, leaving ½ inch of edges uncovered. Sprinkle cheese mixture over top.

Bake 8 to 10 minutes until edges are crisp and golden and cheese is bubbly and melted. Transfer to serving plates; cut each tortilla into 6 wedges. Sprinkle Red & Green Salsa on wedges, if desired.

Red & Green Salsa

1 small red bell pepper
¼ cup coarsely chopped cilantro
3 green onions, cut into thin slices
2 fresh jalapeño chilies, seeded and minced*
2 tablespoons fresh lime juice
1 clove garlic, minced
¼ teaspoon salt

Cut bell pepper lengthwise in half; remove and discard seeds and vein. Cut halves lengthwise into thin slivers; cut slivers crosswise into halves. Mix all ingredients in small bowl. Let stand, covered, at room temperature 1 to 2 hours to blend flavors. *Makes 1 cup*

When working with jalapeño chilies, wear plastic disposable gloves and use caution to prevent irritation of skin or eyes.

Mexican Pizza

Easy Vegetable Squares

Meanwhile, blend cream cheese, mayonnaise, dill weed and salad dressing mix in small bowl. Spread evenly over crust. Sprinkle with desired toppings, then shredded cheese. To serve, cut into squares.

*Favorite recipe from **Wisconsin Milk Marketing Board © 1993***

EASY VEGETABLE SQUARES

Makes 32 appetizers

2 cans (8 ounces each) refrigerated crescent rolls
1 package (8 ounces) cream cheese, softened
1 package (3 ounces) cream cheese, softened
1/3 cup mayonnaise
1 teaspoon dried dill weed, crushed
1 teaspoon buttermilk salad dressing mix
3 cups toppings*
1 cup (4 ounces) shredded Wisconsin Cheddar, Mozzarella or Monterey Jack cheese

Unroll crescent rolls and pat into 15½×10½×1-inch baking pan. Bake according to package directions. Cool on wire rack.

Suggested Toppings: Finely chopped broccoli, cauliflower or green pepper; seeded and chopped tomato; thinly sliced green onion, ripe olives or celery; shredded carrot.

MINI VEGETARIAN PIZZAS

Makes 28 to 30 mini pizzas

FILLING
2 cups drained, chopped ripe tomatoes
1 cup chopped zucchini
¼ cup chopped green onions
1 clove garlic, minced
1 teaspoon salt
1 teaspoon dried oregano leaves, crushed
⅛ teaspoon pepper

DOUGH
3 cups all-purpose flour, divided
1 package (¼ ounce) fast-rising dry yeast
1 teaspoon salt
1 cup water
2 tablespoons olive oil
⅓ cup crushed thin Norwegian crispbread (5 crackers)
Cornmeal (optional)
2 cups shredded Jarlsberg cheese

To make filling: Combine tomatoes, zucchini, green onions, garlic and seasonings in medium bowl. Cover and chill until ready to use; drain, if necessary.

To prepare dough: Mix 2 cups flour, yeast and salt in large bowl. Heat water and oil in small saucepan until temperature reaches 125° to 130°F. Stir into flour mixture along with crispbread crumbs. Add only enough remaining 1 cup flour to make a stiff dough. Knead on lightly floured board until smooth and elastic, about 5 minutes. Cover; let rest 10 minutes in warm place.

Grease two baking sheets. Sprinkle lightly with cornmeal, if desired. Preheat oven to 450°F. Divide dough in half. Roll out one half to ¼-inch thickness. With 2½-inch cookie cutter, cut out 14 to 15 rounds. Place on prepared baking sheets. Repeat with remaining dough. With fingers, press down gently in middle of each round to make indentation. Sprinkle 1 cup cheese evenly over rounds. Spoon about 1 tablespoon drained filling into each center. Sprinkle with remaining 1 cup cheese. Bake 7 to 8 minutes or until cheese is melted and pizzas are heated through.

To knead dough, fold dough in half toward you and press dough away from you with heels of hands. Give dough a quarter turn and continue folding, pushing and turning.

Favorite recipe from **Norseland Foods, Inc.**

QUICK CANTONIZZA

Makes 10 to 12 appetizer servings

- **1 can (10 oz.) refrigerated pizza dough**
- **⅓ cup KIKKOMAN® Sweet & Sour Sauce**
- **1 small green bell pepper, cut into thin rings**
- **2 ounces cooked ham, cut into strips**
- **1 cup (4 oz.) shredded mozzarella cheese**

Prepare pizza dough according to package directions for 12-inch pizza. Spread sweet & sour sauce evenly on dough. Arrange green pepper over sauce, then ham; top with cheese. Bake in 425°F. oven according to package directions. Serve immediately.

PIZZA RICE CAKES

Makes 6 appetizer servings

- **6 rice cakes**
- **⅓ cup pizza sauce**
- **¼ cup sliced ripe olives**
- **¼ cup diced green pepper**
- **¼ cup (about 1 ounce) sliced fresh mushrooms**
- **¼ cup (1 ounce) shredded mozzarella cheese**

Place rice cakes on baking sheet. Spread pizza sauce evenly on each rice cake; top with remaining ingredients. Bake at 400°F. for 10 minutes. Serve immediately.

Microwave Directions: Prepare rice cakes as directed on microproof baking sheet or plate. Cook, uncovered, on HIGH 1½ minutes; rotate after 1 minute. Serve immediately.

Tip: Makes a quick and easy after school snack; great for quick lunches, too!

Favorite recipe from **USA Rice Council**

Quick Cantonizza

MEAT-ZAS!

Satisfy a hearty appetite with these savory pizza pies—for meat lovers only. Let zesty sausage, zippy pepperoni, flavorful ground beef and tasty ham spice up your dinner tonight!

ITALIAN PIZZA CALZONES

Makes 8 calzones

½ **pound Italian sausage**
1 **(26-ounce) jar CLASSICO®**
   D'Abruzzi (Beef & Pork)
   Pasta Sauce
1 **cup sliced fresh mushrooms**
½ **cup chopped green bell pepper**
½ **cup chopped onion**
2 **(8-ounce) packages refrigerated**
   crescent rolls
1 **egg, beaten**
1 **tablespoon water**
1 **cup (4 ounces) shredded**
   mozzarella cheese

Preheat oven to 350°F. In large skillet, brown sausage; pour off fat. Add ¾ *cup* pasta sauce, mushrooms, green pepper and onion; simmer uncovered 10 minutes. Meanwhile, unroll crescent roll dough; separate into 8 rectangles. Firmly press perforations together and flatten slightly. In small bowl, mix egg and water; brush on dough edges. Stir cheese into meat mixture. Spoon equal amounts of meat mixture on half of each rectangle to within ½ inch of edges. Fold dough over filling; press to seal edges. Arrange on baking sheet; brush with egg mixture. Bake 15 minutes or until golden brown. Heat remaining pasta sauce; serve with calzones. Refrigerate leftovers.

QUICK CLASSIC PIZZA

Makes one 12-inch pizza

1 **(12-inch) Italian bread shell or**
   prepared pizza crust
1 **cup (4 ounces) shredded**
   mozzarella cheese
1 **(14-ounce) jar CLASSICO® Pasta**
   Sauce, any flavor (1½ cups)
   Pizza toppings: chopped onion,
   peppers, sliced mushrooms,
   pepperoni, sliced olives,
   cooked sausage, cooked
   ground beef, cooked bacon

Preheat oven to 450°F. Top bread shell with half the cheese, pasta sauce, desired toppings and remaining cheese. Bake 10 to 12 minutes or until hot and bubbly. Let stand 5 minutes. Serve warm. Refrigerate leftovers.

Top to bottom: Quick Classic Pizza, Italian Pizza Calzone and Meatza Pizza Pie (page 22)

Fast and Easy Pizza

HOT CHILI PIZZA

Makes 6 to 8 servings

1 tablespoon vegetable oil
1 medium onion, chopped
1 clove garlic, minced
2 tablespoons chili powder
1 pound ground beef
1 can (16 ounces) tomatoes, undrained
1 teaspoon salt
1/2 teaspoon celery seed
1/4 teaspoon ground cumin
1/2 teaspoon TABASCO® Brand Pepper Sauce
1 pound unbaked dough for pizza
1 avocado, peeled and sliced
1 red or Spanish onion, thinly sliced and separated into rings
1 1/2 cups shredded Monterey Jack cheese

Preheat oven to 450°F. In large skillet heat oil. Add onion, garlic and chili powder; cook 5 minutes or until onion is tender. Add ground beef; break up with fork and cook until lightly browned. Pour off fat. Add tomatoes, salt, celery seed, cumin and Tabasco® sauce. Simmer 5 minutes; remove from heat.

Pat, stretch or roll pizza dough to fit lightly greased 15×11-inch jelly-roll pan. Spread meat mixture over dough. Bake 10 minutes. Remove from oven. Arrange avocado slices and onion rings over top; sprinkle with cheese. Return to oven; bake 5 minutes longer or until crust is light brown and cheese is melted.

FAST AND EASY PIZZA

Makes 8 servings

1 pound French bread loaf (approximately 18×5-inch), split horizontally and toasted
1 1/2 cups (15-ounce bottle) CONTADINA® Pizza Squeeze Pizza Sauce, divided
2 to 3 cups of assorted pizza toppings: shredded cheeses; sliced or chopped pepperoni, ham, bell peppers, mushrooms, olives, onions, green onions; cooked crumbled Italian sausage or ground beef; pineapple chunks; CONTADINA® Italian-Style Pear-Shaped Tomatoes, drained, cut into chunks

Place French bread halves on cookie sheet or broiler pan. Spread each half with approximately *3/4 cup* pizza sauce. Arrange desired toppings over sauce. Bake in preheated 350°F. oven for 10 to 12 minutes or until topping is heated through. Slice each half into 4 servings.

SAUSAGE PINEAPPLE PIZZA

Makes 4 to 6 servings

2 cans (8 ounces each) DOLE®
   Crushed Pineapple in Juice
½ cup bottled pizza sauce
1 clove garlic, pressed
1 teaspoon dried oregano leaves,
   crumbled
½ loaf frozen bread dough,
   thawed
½ cup chopped DOLE® Green Bell
   Pepper
¼ cup sliced DOLE® Green Onion
½ pound Italian sausage,*
   crumbled, cooked and
   drained
2 cups (8 ounces) shredded
   mozzarella or Cheddar
   cheese
2 tablespoons grated Parmesan
   cheese

• Drain pineapple well; press out excess juice with back of spoon.

• Combine pizza sauce, garlic and oregano. Roll thawed dough on floured board to fit 12-inch pizza pan or 13×9-inch baking pan. Press dough into greased pan. If using 13×9-inch pan, press dough 1 inch up sides of pan to resemble deep-dish pizza.

• Spread dough with pizza sauce mixture. Top with green pepper, onion, sausage, pineapple and cheeses.

• Bake in 500°F oven 12 to 15 minutes until crust is browned.

Or use 1 cup julienne ham strips; 8 slices bacon, diced, partially cooked; or 5 breakfast sausage links, cooked, cubed.

Prep time: 15 minutes
Bake time: 15 minutes

"NO DOUGH" PIZZA

Makes 6 servings

2 cups Wheat CHEX® brand
   cereal, crushed to 1 cup
1 pound lean ground beef
1 egg, beaten
1 cup prepared pizza sauce *or*
   spaghetti sauce, divided
¼ cup grated Parmesan cheese
1½ teaspoons Italian seasoning
1 cup (4 ounces) shredded
   mozzarella cheese
   Favorite pizza toppings
   (optional)

Preheat oven to 375°F. In medium bowl combine cereal, meat, egg, ¼ cup sauce, Parmesan cheese and seasoning; add ½ teaspoon salt and ¼ teaspoon pepper if desired. Press mixture onto ungreased 12-inch pizza pan to form a "crust." Bake 10 minutes. Remove from oven and top with remaining ¾ cup sauce, mozzarella cheese and pizza toppings if desired. Return to oven for an additional 10 to 15 minutes or until cheese is melted.

Sausage Pineapple Pizza

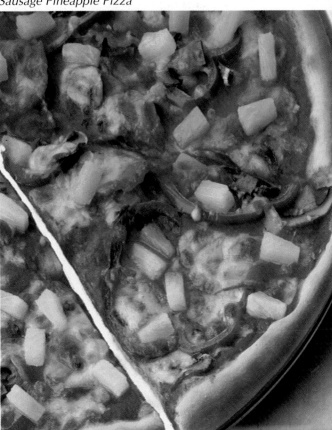

JARLSBERG PIZZA

Makes 6 to 8 servings

1/2 loaf (1/2 pound) frozen pizza
    dough, thawed
4 cups shredded Jarlsberg cheese,
    divided
3 cups chopped broccoli
2 tablespoons oil
1/4 teaspoon dried oregano leaves,
    crushed
1 cup sliced pepperoni

Preheat oven to 475°F. On lightly floured board, roll out dough to fit 12-inch pizza pan. Press into pan; crimp edges to form rim. Top with 2 cups cheese. Sprinkle with broccoli, oil and oregano. Top with remaining 2 cups cheese and pepperoni. Bake 12 minutes or until crust is golden.

Favorite recipe from **Norseland Foods, Inc.**

STUFFED ITALIAN PIZZA PIE

Makes 6 servings

1/2 pound lean ground beef
1/2 cup chopped onion
1/2 cup chopped green bell pepper
1 clove garlic, finely chopped
1/2 cup CLASSICO® Di Napoli
    (Tomato & Basil) Pasta Sauce
2 teaspoons WYLER'S® or
    STEERO® Beef-Flavor Instant
    Bouillon
1 teaspoon Italian seasoning
2 (8-ounce) packages refrigerated
    crescent rolls
1 (4-ounce) can sliced
    mushrooms, drained
1 cup (4 ounces) shredded
    mozzarella cheese

Preheat oven to 400°F. In large skillet, brown meat with onion, green pepper and garlic; pour off fat. Add pasta sauce, bouillon and seasoning. Simmer uncovered 10 to 15 minutes. Meanwhile, unroll 1 package crescent roll dough; separate into 8 triangles. On 12-inch pizza pan, arrange triangles in circle; press into pan, sealing edges and forming 1/4-inch rim. Spoon meat sauce over crust; top with mushrooms and cheese. Separate remaining dough into 8 triangles. Arrange triangles spoke-fashion over filling with points toward center. Do not seal outer edges of triangles to bottom crust. Bake 15 to 20 minutes or until golden brown. Refrigerate leftovers.

MEATZA PIZZA PIE

Makes one 9-inch pie

1 pound ground round
1/2 cup fresh bread crumbs (1 slice)
1 egg
2 teaspoons WYLER'S® or
    STEERO® Beef-Flavor Instant
    Bouillon
1/2 teaspoon Italian seasoning
1/2 cup CLASSICO® Di Napoli
    (Tomato & Basil) Pasta Sauce
1 (2 1/2-ounce) jar sliced
    mushrooms, drained
2 tablespoons chopped green bell
    pepper
2 tablespoons chopped onion
1 cup (4 ounces) shredded
    mozzarella cheese

Preheat oven to 350°F. In medium bowl, combine meat, crumbs, egg, bouillon and seasoning; mix well. Press evenly on bottom and up side to rim of 9-inch pie plate to form crust. Bake 15 minutes; pour off fat. Spoon pasta sauce over crust. Top with mushrooms, green pepper, onion and cheese. Bake 10 minutes longer or until cheese melts. Garnish as desired. Refrigerate leftovers.

Deli Stuffed Calzone

DELI STUFFED CALZONE

Makes 8 servings

1¾ cups (14.5-ounce can) CONTADINA® Recipe Ready Tomatoes, well drained

1¼ cups (10-ounce package) frozen chopped spinach, thawed and squeezed dry

¾ cup (3 ounces) thinly sliced pepperoni, chopped

¾ cup (3 ounces) thinly sliced salami, chopped

1 cup (4 ounces) shredded mozzarella cheese

1 cup ricotta cheese

½ cup chopped Spanish olives stuffed with pimiento

⅓ cup grated Parmesan cheese

1½ teaspoons garlic powder

1½ teaspoons dried basil leaves, crushed

1½ teaspoons dried oregano leaves, crushed

1 teaspoon seasoned pepper

2 loaves (1 pound each) frozen bread dough, thawed

2 tablespoons olive oil

In large bowl, combine tomatoes, spinach, pepperoni, salami, mozzarella cheese, ricotta cheese, olives, Parmesan cheese, garlic powder, basil, oregano and pepper; set aside filling. Cut each bread loaf in half. On lightly floured board, roll one bread dough half into 12-inch circle. Place on pizza pan. Spread 1⅓ cups of filling on half of dough circle to within ½ inch of edge. Fold dough over filling making half circle. Press edges with fork to seal. Cut 3 slits in dough to allow steam to escape. Repeat process making 3 more calzones. Bake in preheated 350°F. oven for 20 minutes. Brush with olive oil. Bake an additional 5 to 10 minutes or until golden brown. Let stand 10 minutes before cutting.

EASY BEEF PIZZA

Makes 4 servings

- ½ **pound ground beef (80% lean)**
  Quick Pizza Crust
  (recipe follows)
- 1 **teaspoon dried Italian seasoning**
- ¼ **teaspoon fennel seeds, crushed**
- ¼ **teaspoon crushed dried red**
  pepper
- 1 **can (8 ounces) pizza sauce**
- 1 **medium green bell pepper, cut**
  into thin rings
- 1 **green onion, sliced**
- ¾ **cup (6 ounces) shredded**
  mozzarella cheese
- ¼ **cup grated Parmesan cheese**

Prepare Quick Pizza Crust. Preheat oven to 450°F. Heat large skillet over medium heat until hot. Crumble beef into skillet. Cook, stirring to separate meat, until no pink remains. Pour off drippings. Sprinkle Italian seasoning, fennel seeds and crushed red pepper over beef. Spread pizza sauce over baked pizza crust. Place green pepper and onion over sauce; top with beef mixture. Sprinkle with mozzarella and Parmesan cheeses. Bake 7 to 10 minutes or until cheese is melted.

Quick Pizza Crust

- 1¾ **to 2 cups flour, divided**
- 1 **package (¼ ounce) fast-rising**
  dry yeast
- 2 **teaspoons sugar**
- ½ **teaspoon salt**
- ⅔ **cup warm water**
  (105° to 115°F)
- 1½ **teaspoons vegetable oil**
  Cornmeal

Combine 1 cup flour, yeast, sugar and salt in large bowl. Stir in water and oil. Add enough remaining flour to form soft dough. Turn out onto lightly floured surface; knead* 5 minutes or until smooth and elastic. Cover; let rest 10 minutes. Preheat oven to 350°F. Shape or roll dough into 12-inch circle. Sprinkle cornmeal on lightly greased 12-inch pizza pan or baking sheet. Place dough on pan, pressing gently to fit. Bake 10 minutes or until golden brown.

To knead dough, fold dough in half toward you and press dough away from you with heels of hands. Give dough a quarter turn and continue folding, pushing and turning.

Favorite recipe from **National Live Stock and Meat Board**

SPICY PEPPERONI PIZZA

Makes 4 servings

- 4 **(6-inch) prepared, pre-baked**
  pizza crusts
- 1 **can (14½ ounces)**
  DEL MONTE® Pizza Style
  Chunky Tomatoes
- 2 **cups shredded mozzarella**
  cheese
- 2 **ounces sliced pepperoni**
- 8 **pitted ripe olives, sliced**
- 2 **tablespoons sliced green onions**

Preheat oven to 450°F. Place crusts on baking sheet. Spread tomatoes evenly over crusts. Layer ½ of cheese, then the pepperoni, olives and green onions. Top with remaining cheese. Bake 6 to 8 minutes or until hot and bubbly.

Prep time: 7 minutes
Cook time: 8 minutes

Easy Beef Pizza

Stuffed Pizza

On floured surface, roll bread dough into two 12-inch circles. Place one circle on greased baking sheet. Spread with ¼ *cup* pizza sauce to 1 inch from edge. In large bowl, combine pepperoni, spinach, mozzarella, ricotta, *1 cup* Parmesan cheese and olives. Spread mixture over pizza sauce. Squeeze ¼ *cup* pizza sauce evenly over filling; dampen outside edge. Place remaining bread dough on top and seal. Cut 8 steam vents. Bake on lowest rack in preheated 350°F. oven for 20 minutes. Brush with olive oil; sprinkle with *1 tablespoon* Parmesan cheese. Bake for additional 15 to 20 minutes or until well browned. Let stand 15 minutes before cutting. Warm *remaining* pizza sauce and serve over wedges of pizza.

STUFFED PIZZA

Makes 8 servings

    2 loaves (1 pound each) frozen
        bread dough, thawed
1¾ cups (15-ounce bottle)
        CONTADINA® Pizza Squeeze
        Pizza Sauce, divided
    1 package (3 ounces) sliced
        pepperoni, quartered
1¼ cups (10-ounce package) frozen
        chopped spinach, thawed and
        squeezed dry
    1 cup (4 ounces) shredded
        mozzarella cheese
    1 cup (8-ounce carton) ricotta
        cheese
    1 cup grated Parmesan cheese
    1 cup (3.8-ounce can) sliced ripe
        olives, drained
    1 tablespoon olive oil
    1 tablespoon grated Parmesan
        cheese

MEXICALI PIZZA

Makes 4 servings

        Vegetable oil
    2 large flour tortillas *or* 4 small
        flour tortillas
    1 pound ground beef
    1 package (1.25 ounces)
        LAWRY'S® Taco Spices &
        Seasonings
  ¾ cup water
1½ cups (6 ounces) grated
        Monterey Jack or Cheddar
        cheese
    3 tablespoons diced green chiles
    2 medium tomatoes, sliced
    1 can (2¼ ounces) sliced ripe
        olives, drained
  ½ cup salsa

In large skillet, pour oil to ¼ inch depth; heat. (For small tortillas, use small skillet.) Fry each tortilla about 5 seconds. While still pliable, turn tortilla over. Fry until golden brown. (Edges of tortilla should turn up about ½ inch.) Drain well on paper towels. In medium skillet, brown ground beef until crumbly; drain fat. Add Taco Spices & Seasonings and water; blend well. Bring to a boil; reduce heat and simmer, uncovered, 5 minutes. Place fried tortillas on pizza pan. Layer taco meat, ½ of cheese, chiles, tomatoes, remaining ½ of cheese, olives and salsa. Bake, uncovered, in 425°F oven 15 minutes for large pizzas or 7 to 8 minutes for small pizzas.

Presentation: For large pizza, cut in wedges for serving. Small pizzas may be cut in half or left whole.

Hint: One pound ground turkey or 1½ cups shredded, cooked chicken can be used in place of beef.

Pasta Pizza

PASTA PIZZA

Makes 8 servings

- 2 cups uncooked corkscrew macaroni
- 3 beaten eggs
- ½ cup milk
- ½ cup (2 ounces) shredded Wisconsin Cheddar cheese
- ¼ cup finely chopped onion
- 1 pound lean ground beef
- 1 (15-ounce) can tomato sauce
- 1 teaspoon dried basil leaves, crushed
- 1 teaspoon dried oregano leaves, crushed
- ½ teaspoon garlic salt
- 1 medium tomato, thinly sliced
- 1 green bell pepper, sliced into rings
- ¼ cup sliced ripe olives
- 1½ cups (6 ounces) shredded Wisconsin Mozzarella cheese

Cook macaroni according to package directions; drain well.

Preheat oven to 350°F. Combine eggs and milk in large bowl; stir into cooked macaroni. Stir in Cheddar cheese and onion; mix well. Spread macaroni mixture evenly over well-buttered 14-inch pizza pan. Bake 25 minutes.

Meanwhile, heat large skillet over medium heat until hot. Crumble beef into skillet. Cook, stirring to separate meat, until no pink remains. Drain off fat. Stir in tomato sauce, basil, oregano and garlic salt. Spoon meat mixture over baked macaroni crust. Arrange tomato slices, green pepper rings and olives over meat mixture. Sprinkle with Mozzarella cheese. Bake 15 minutes longer or until cheese is bubbly.

Favorite recipe from **Wisconsin Milk Marketing Board** © 1993

Camper's Pizza

CAMPER'S PIZZA

Makes 4 servings

3/4 **pound ground beef**
1 **medium onion, chopped**
1/2 **teaspoon salt**
1 **can (8 ounces) refrigerated crescent rolls**
1 **can (8 ounces) pizza sauce**
1 **can (4 ounces) mushroom stems and pieces, drained and chopped**
1 **can (2 1/4 ounces) pitted sliced ripe olives, drained**
1/3 **cup coarsely chopped green bell pepper**
1 **cup (4 ounces) shredded mozzarella cheese**
1 **teaspoon dried oregano leaves, crushed**

Crumble beef into well-seasoned 11- to 12-inch cast-iron skillet over *medium* coals.* Add onion; cook beef and onion, stirring to separate meat, until no pink remains. Remove beef mixture with slotted spoon to paper towels; season with salt. Pour off drippings from pan. *Do not clean skillet.* Separate crescent roll dough into triangles; place in same skillet, points toward center, to form circle. Press edges together to form bottom crust and 1-inch rim up side of skillet. Spread 1/2 of pizza sauce over dough; spoon beef mixture over sauce. Top with mushrooms, olives and green pepper. Pour remaining sauce over all; sprinkle with cheese and oregano. Place skillet in center of grid over medium coals. Place cover on cooker;** cook 20 to 30 minutes or until crust is lightly browned.

To test coals, hold hand, palm side down, just above grid. If you can keep your hand in place before pulling away for a 4-second count, coals are medium.

**If cooked over open grill or coals, cover pan securely with foil.*

Favorite recipe from **National Live Stock and Meat Board**

GREEK-STYLE PIZZAS

Makes 4 servings

1 cup Basic Pizza Sauce (page 47)
1 teaspoon dried oregano leaves, crushed
4 pita bread rounds
1 can (14 ounces) artichoke hearts, drained and cut into fourths
4 ounces canned ham, cut into julienne strips
½ cup sliced onion
1 can (2 ounces) anchovies, drained (optional)
8 pitted ripe olives, sliced
½ cup crumbled feta cheese

Prepare Basic Pizza Sauce. Preheat broiler. Mix Basic Pizza Sauce and oregano; spread on pita breads. Arrange artichoke hearts, ham, onion, anchovies, if desired, and olives evenly over sauce; sprinkle with cheese. Broil 3 minutes or until cheese is melted.

Prep time: 10 minutes

Favorite recipe from **Canned Food Information Council**

BREAKFAST PINEAPPLE PIZZAS

Makes 5 servings

1 can (20 ounces) DOLE® Pineapple Tidbits in Juice
½ cup bottled pizza sauce
1 teaspoon dried oregano leaves, crumbled
5 English muffins, split and toasted
10 slices DOLE® Green Bell Pepper
10 slices bacon, halved and cooked
1¼ cups shredded Cheddar or mozzarella cheese

• Drain pineapple; reserve 1 cup pineapple for garnish.

• Combine pizza sauce and oregano in small bowl.

• Top each muffin half evenly with pizza sauce mixture, bell pepper, bacon, pineapple and cheese.

• Broil or bake in 500°F oven 2 to 4 minutes or until cheese melts.

• Top each with reserved pineapple.

Prep time: 20 minutes
Bake time: 4 minutes

HAM AND CHEESE CALZONE

Makes 1 serving

Vegetable cooking spray
½ cup chopped red bell pepper
½ cup chopped yellow or green bell pepper
¼ cup sliced mushrooms
1 garlic clove, minced
1 (6-inch) pita bread
1 ounce lean ham, cut in strips
1 ounce shredded Jarlsberg or Jarlsberg Lite cheese
1 tablespoon chopped parsley
1 tablespoon grated Parmesan cheese
Ground black pepper

Preheat oven to 350°F. Coat small skillet with vegetable cooking spray. Heat over medium-high heat until hot. Add peppers, mushrooms and garlic; cook and stir until soft. Make slit in pita bread; fill with bell pepper mixture, ham, Jarlsberg cheese and parsley. Sprinkle with Parmesan cheese; season with black pepper to taste. Wrap in foil; bake 15 minutes or until golden brown.

Tip: You can double the recipe and freeze second calzone for up to 1 week.

Favorite recipe from **Norseland Foods, Inc.**

SNAPPY BEAN PIZZA

Makes 1 (14-inch) pizza

1 **cup dried Idaho red, pinto or pink beans**
  Water
1 **teaspoon salt**
1 **tablespoon olive oil**
1 **cup chopped onion**
2 **cloves garlic, minced**
1 **can (8 ounces) tomato sauce**
1/2 **teaspoon dried oregano leaves, crushed**
1/8 **teaspoon ground cayenne pepper**
1 **package (16 ounces) hot roll mix**
1 **green bell pepper, cut into rings**
1/4 **cup sliced, pitted ripe olives**
4 **ounces spicy smoked sausage, diced**
2 **cups (8 ounces) shredded Swiss cheese**
2 **tablespoons grated Parmesan cheese**

Rinse beans; add to 5 cups boiling water in large pot. Boil 2 minutes; remove from heat. Cover and soak 12 hours or overnight. (Or, for quick soak method, add beans to 5 cups boiling water; boil 3 minutes and let stand 1 to 4 hours.)

Preheat oven to 400°F. Drain and rinse beans. Add 3 cups water and salt to beans; cover and simmer about 30 to 45 minutes or until tender. Drain and set aside 1/2 cup beans; mash remaining beans. Heat oil in large skillet over medium heat until hot. Add onion and garlic; cook and stir until soft. Add mashed beans, tomato sauce, oregano and cayenne pepper. Prepare hot roll mix, following package directions except omit egg. Press dough into oiled 14-inch pizza pan. Crimp edges to form rim. Spread bean mixture on dough. Garnish with green pepper rings. Sprinkle with olives, sausage, remaining 1/2 cup beans and cheeses. Bake 20 minutes or until crust is golden.

Favorite recipe from **Idaho Bean Commission**

PIZZA SONORA

Makes 4 servings

1/2 **pound ground beef**
1/2 **teaspoon ground cumin**
4 **(6-inch) prepared, pre-baked pizza crusts***
1 **can (14 1/2 ounces) DEL MONTE® Pizza Style Chunky Tomatoes**
2 **cups shredded Monterey Jack cheese**
1 **small green pepper, thinly sliced**
1/2 **medium onion, finely chopped (optional)**
1 **can (4 ounces) diced green chiles**

Preheat oven to 450°F. In large skillet, cook meat with cumin; drain. Place crusts on baking sheet. Spread tomatoes evenly over crusts. Top with meat mixture, 1/2 of cheese, pepper, onion, chiles and remaining cheese. Bake 6 to 8 minutes or until hot and bubbly.

*Refrigerated or frozen pizza dough may also be used; prepare and bake according to package directions.

Prep & Cook time: 25 minutes

Pizza Sonora

HAWAIIAN PINEAPPLE PIZZA

Makes 6 to 8 servings

- 1 long loaf (1 pound) French bread
- 1½ cups pizza sauce
- 4 ounces Canadian bacon, slivered
- 1 small DOLE® Green Bell Pepper, sliced
- 1 can (20 ounces) DOLE® Pineapple Tidbits in Juice, drained
- 2 cups shredded mozzarella cheese

- Preheat broiler.

- Cut bread lengthwise. Spread with pizza sauce.

- Top evenly with remaining ingredients.

- Broil until cheese melts.

Prep time: 15 minutes
Cook time: 10 minutes

Hawaiian Pineapple Pizza

CHICAGO DEEP-DISH BEEF PIZZA

Makes 6 servings

- 1 package (¼ ounce) active dry yeast
- ¾ cup warm water (105° to 115°F)
- 1 teaspoon sugar
- 1 teaspoon salt, divided
- 2 tablespoons olive oil
- 2 to 2¼ cups quick-mixing flour Cornmeal
- ½ to 1 pound lean ground round
- 2 cloves garlic, peeled and crushed
- 3 cups shredded Jarlsberg cheese, divided
- 1½ to 2 cups canned tomato sauce
- 1 small green pepper, sliced
- 1 can (4 ounces) sliced mushrooms, drained

In large bowl, dissolve yeast in water. Stir in sugar, ¾ teaspoon salt and olive oil. Add 1 cup flour and beat until smooth. Mix in remaining flour until dough forms. Turn out onto lightly floured surface; knead 1 minute.

Grease heavy 10½- to 12-inch skillet with ovenproof handle or 13×9-inch metal baking pan. Sprinkle lightly with cornmeal. Roll dough out 1½ inches larger than skillet; press into bottom and up sides. Cover; let rise 30 minutes.

Preheat oven to 425°F. Heat small skillet over medium heat until hot. Crumble beef into skillet. Add garlic and remaining ¼ teaspoon salt; cook 7 minutes, stirring to separate meat, or until no pink remains. Drain well. Spread 2 cups cheese over bottom of crust. Top with beef mixture; drizzle with tomato sauce. Arrange green pepper and mushrooms on tomato sauce. Sprinkle with remaining

1 cup cheese. Bake 20 to 25 minutes or until cheese is melted and crust is lightly browned. Let stand on wire rack 10 minutes.

Sausage Pizza: Prepare dough as directed above. Omit beef and remaining ¼ teaspoon salt. Cook ½ pound bulk (country-style) pork sausage with garlic as above; drain. Assemble and bake as directed.

Pepperoni Pizza: Prepare dough as directed above. Omit beef, garlic and remaining ¼ teaspoon salt. Cut 5 ounces of pepperoni into ¼-inch slices. Assemble and bake as directed.

Favorite recipe from **Norseland Foods, Inc.**

Beef Pizza Crisp

BEEF PIZZA CRISP

Makes 4 servings

12 ounces ground beef (80% lean)
1 package (¼ ounce) active dry
**   yeast**
¼ cup warm water
**   (105° to 115°F)**
1 teaspoon salt, divided
½ teaspoon sugar
⅔ to ¾ cup all-purpose flour
1 large tomato, peeled, seeded
**   and chopped**
1 tablespoon sliced green onion
½ to ¾ teaspoon dried oregano
**   leaves, crushed**
⅛ teaspoon crushed dried red
**   pepper**
1 cup (4 ounces) finely shredded
**   part-skim mozzarella cheese**
1 tablespoon grated Parmesan
**   cheese**

Dissolve yeast in water in large bowl; stir in ½ teaspoon salt, sugar and ⅔ cup flour. Add remaining flour to form soft dough. Turn out on lightly floured surface. Knead* until smooth and elastic. Cover; let rest 10 minutes. Roll dough into 12-inch circle; place on baking sheet. Crimp edges to form rim. Cover; let rise 30 minutes.

Preheat oven to 400°F. Bake 4 to 5 minutes. Meanwhile, cook and stir tomato and onion in large skillet over medium-high heat 2 minutes; drain and set aside. Crumble ground beef into same skillet. Cook, stirring to separate meat, until no pink remains. Pour off drippings. Sprinkle remaining ½ teaspoon salt, oregano, to taste, and crushed red pepper over beef. Stir in mozzarella cheese and reserved tomato mixture; spoon evenly over crust. Sprinkle with Parmesan cheese; bake 6 to 7 minutes longer or until heated through and crust is brown.

*To knead dough, fold in half toward you and press dough away from you with heels of hands. Give dough a quarter turn and continue folding, pushing and turning.

Favorite recipe from **National Live Stock and Meat Board**

TWO-COURSE PIZZA FOR TWO

Makes 2 (2-course) servings

1 **can (10 ounces) refrigerated pizza crust**
6 **ounces pizza sauce**
¼ **cup apricot preserves**
2 **ounces prosciutto or cooked ham, cut into strips**
¼ **cup (1 ounce) *each* shredded Wisconsin Cheddar, Muenster and Provolone cheese**
¼ **cup (1 ounce) grated Wisconsin Parmesan cheese**
2 **ounces artichoke hearts, cut into ⅛-inch-thick slices**
5 **ounces Wisconsin Brie cheese, cut into ⅛-inch-thick slices**
1 **large Granny Smith apple, cored, cut into ⅛-inch-thick slices and halved**
2 **tablespoons toasted pine nuts (optional)**
2 **tablespoons cinnamon sugar**

Unroll pizza crust and press into 12-inch pizza pan. Crimp edges to form rim. Preheat oven to 425°F. Spread pizza sauce over ½ of crust. Spread apricot preserves over the other half. Arrange prosciutto over pizza sauce. Combine Cheddar, Muenster, Provolone and Parmesan cheeses in small bowl; sprinkle cheese blend over prosciutto. Arrange artichoke hearts neatly on top of cheese.

Place 1 slice of Brie at center of apricot side of crust; arrange remaining Brie slices in a semicircle over crust. Layer apple slices on top of Brie. Sprinkle pine nuts, if desired, over apples. Sprinkle cinnamon sugar over apples. Bake 15 to 20 minutes or until crust is browned and cheese is bubbly and golden. Allow pizza to rest for 5 minutes before slicing.

Tip: Two 6-inch pizzas, one for main-course and one for dessert, can be made instead of one 12-inch pizza. Unroll pizza dough and press into two (6-inch) circles on baking sheet.

Favorite recipe from **Wisconsin Milk Marketing Board © 1993**

SMOKY PINEAPPLE PIZZA

Makes 4 servings

1 **(12-inch) prepared pizza crust**
½ **cup bottled pizza sauce**
¼ **pound cooked ham, diced**
½ **DOLE® Green Bell Pepper, diced**
3 **DOLE® Green Onions, diced**
1½ **cups (6 ounces) shredded smoked Cheddar cheese**
1 **can (8 ounces) DOLE® Pineapple Tidbits in Juice, drained**

• Spread crust with pizza sauce. Top with ham, green pepper, onions, cheese and pineapple.

• Bake in 425°F oven 20 minutes or until cheese is melted and pizza is heated through.

Prep time: 20 minutes
Bake time: 20 minutes

Calzone

CALZONE

Makes 3 large calzones

- 1 **cup warm water (105° to 115°F)**
- ½ **teaspoon sugar**
- 1 **package (¼ ounce) active dry yeast**
- 3 **cups sifted all-purpose flour, divided**
- 2 **tablespoons oil**
- ½ **teaspoon salt**
- 12 **ounces mozzarella cheese, shredded or diced**
- 6 **ounces creamy goat cheese**
- 3 **ounces sliced prosciutto or cooked ham, cut into strips**
- 3 **tablespoons chopped chives**
- 1 **tablespoon finely minced fresh garlic**
- 2 **tablespoons grated Parmesan cheese**

Combine water and sugar in large bowl; sprinkle with yeast. Let stand 5 minutes to soften. Add 1½ cups flour; beat with electric mixer until smooth. Stir in oil and salt. Gradually blend in enough of remaining flour with wooden spoon to make moderately stiff dough. Turn out onto lightly floured surface; knead until smooth. Return to bowl; cover and let rise in warm place until doubled. Punch down dough; divide into 3 equal portions. Roll one portion on lightly floured surface to 9-inch circle. Place ⅓ of mozzarella on one side of dough; dot with ⅓ of goat cheese and top with ⅓ of prosciutto. Repeat with remaining dough, cheeses and prosciutto. Mix chives and garlic; sprinkle over filling. Moisten edges of dough with water and fold over to enclose filling, pressing edges firmly together. Place on lightly greased baking sheets. Let rise 30 to 45 minutes or until dough feels light to the touch. Cut slit in each calzone to allow steam to escape. Preheat oven to 375°F. Bake 30 to 35 minutes or until browned. Remove from oven; brush tops with oil. Sprinkle each with 2 teaspoons grated Parmesan cheese. Serve warm.

Favorite recipe from **Fresh Garlic Association**

HAWAIIAN PIZZA WITH HAM AND PINEAPPLE

Makes 4 servings

1 can (8 ounces) DEL MONTE® Sliced Pineapple In Its Own Juice
1 can (6 ounces) DEL MONTE® Tomato Paste
2 tablespoons chopped onion
1/2 teaspoon dried oregano, crushed
1/2 teaspoon dried basil, crushed
1/2 teaspoon salt
1/4 teaspoon sugar
1 clove garlic, crushed
Dash black pepper
1 (16-ounce) ready-made pizza crust*
2 cups shredded mozzarella cheese
3 slices cooked ham, cut in 1/2-inch strips
1 green pepper, sliced into rings
1/3 cup grated Parmesan cheese

Preheat oven to 400°F. Drain pineapple reserving juice. Combine reserved juice with tomato paste, onion, oregano, basil, salt, sugar, garlic and black pepper; mix well. Spread over crust. Sprinkle with mozzarella cheese. Arrange pineapple, ham and green pepper on top. Sprinkle with Parmesan cheese. Place on baking sheet. Bake 8 to 10 minutes or until hot and bubbly.

Refrigerated or frozen pizza dough may also be used; prepare and bake according to package directions.

BRANIZZA

Makes 18 slices

1 1/2 cups KELLOGG'S® ALL-BRAN® cereal
1 1/2 pounds lean ground round
2 egg whites, slightly beaten
1/4 cup skim milk
1 cup chopped onions
2 teaspoons Italian seasoning
1 can (8 ounces) tomato sauce with Italian seasoning
1 can (8 ounces) pizza sauce
2 cups (8 ounces) shredded part-skim mozzarella cheese
1 large green bell pepper, thinly sliced
1 can (2 1/4 ounces) sliced ripe olives, drained (optional)
1/2 cup grated Parmesan cheese

1. In a large bowl, combine Kellogg's® All-Bran® cereal, beef, egg whites, milk, onions and seasoning. Let stand 5 minutes or until cereal is softened.

2. Evenly press meat mixture into an 15×11×2-inch baking pan. Stir together tomato and pizza sauces; spread over meat mixture. Sprinkle sauce with mozzarella cheese, pepper slices, olives, if desired, and Parmesan cheese.

3. Bake at 400°F about 30 minutes or until cheese is bubbly and edges begin to brown. Cut into 18 slices. Serve hot.

Note: To freeze Branizza, individually wrap slices in plastic wrap. Keep in freezer up to 3 weeks. Thaw in refrigerator before reheating.

Hawaiian Pizza with Ham and Pineapple

BARBECUE PIZZA

Makes 1 (16-inch) pizza

- 1 package ($\frac{1}{4}$ ounce) active dry yeast
- 1 cup warm water (105° to 115°F), divided
- 3$\frac{1}{2}$ cups all-purpose flour
- 1 teaspoon salt
- $\frac{1}{4}$ cup olive oil
- 2 cups prepared barbecue sauce, divided
- 3 cups (12 ounces) shredded Wisconsin Mozzarella (low-moisture, part-skim) cheese
- $\frac{1}{2}$ cup (2 ounces) shredded Wisconsin Pasteurized Process cheese
- 1$\frac{1}{4}$ pounds barbecue meat (cooked and chopped pork shoulder), heated

Dissolve yeast in $\frac{1}{4}$ cup water; set aside. Combine flour and salt in large bowl; make well in center. Add yeast mixture, remaining $\frac{3}{4}$ cup water and oil. Mix with wooden spoon until ball of dough forms.

Turn out onto lightly floured surface. Knead 7 to 8 minutes or until smooth (dust dough with flour if dough is sticky). Place dough in lightly floured large bowl; cover with plastic wrap and clean kitchen towel. Let rise in warm place 1$\frac{1}{2}$ hours or until double in bulk.

Punch down dough and turn out onto lightly floured surface. Knead lightly about 2 minutes. Roll or stretch dough into 16-inch circle, about $\frac{1}{4}$ inch thick. Place dough circle in 16-inch flat pizza pan. Cover with towel; let dough rest about 45 minutes.

Preheat oven to 500°F. Spread $\frac{2}{3}$ cup barbecue sauce evenly over dough to within $\frac{1}{2}$ inch of edge. Mix cheeses; sprinkle over sauce. Bake 10 minutes or until cheese is bubbly. Remove from oven; spread meat over cheese. Pour remaining 1$\frac{1}{3}$ cups barbecue sauce evenly over meat.

Favorite recipe from **Wisconsin Milk Marketing Board** © 1993

Barbecue Pizza

PEPPERONI "PIZZA" CASSEROLE

Makes 8 servings

2 bags UNCLE BEN'S® Rice Boil-
In-Bag Family Servings*
2 eggs
¼ cup (1 ounce) grated Parmesan
cheese
1 teaspoon dried oregano leaves,
crushed
½ teaspoon garlic powder
1 jar (14 to 16 ounces) spaghetti
sauce
3 to 5 ounces sliced pepperoni
1 can (4 ounces) sliced
mushrooms, drained
1 green bell pepper, thinly sliced
into rings
1 package (8 ounces) shredded
mozzarella cheese

Cook rice according to package
directions. Combine rice, eggs,
Parmesan cheese, oregano and
garlic powder; mix well. Spread into
greased 13×9-inch baking pan.
Bake in 350°F. oven 10 minutes or
until firm. Spread spaghetti sauce
over rice mixture; top evenly with
pepperoni, mushrooms, pepper rings
and mozzarella cheese. Bake 15
minutes longer or until hot and
bubbly.

*4 cups cooked Uncle Ben's®
Converted® Brand Rice or Uncle
Ben's® Rice In An Instant may be
substituted.*

Pepperoni "Pizza" Casserole

DEEP-DISH COTTAGE PIZZA

Makes one 15×10-inch pizza

1 (16-ounce) package hot roll mix
½ pound bulk hot Italian sausage
1 clove garlic, finely chopped
1 (16-ounce) container BORDEN®
or MEADOW GOLD'S®
Cottage Cheese
1 (12-ounce) can tomato paste
½ cup chopped onion
1 teaspoon oregano leaves
1 teaspoon salt
½ cup chopped green bell pepper
½ cup grated Parmesan cheese

Prepare roll mix and let rise as
package directs. Press on bottom
and up sides of greased 15×10-inch
baking pan. Let rise 30 minutes. In
skillet, cook sausage and garlic; pour
off fat. In medium bowl, combine
cottage cheese, tomato paste, onion,
oregano and salt; spread in prepared
pan. Top with sausage, green pepper
and grated cheese. Bake in
preheated 375°F oven 35 minutes.
Refrigerate leftovers.

SPICY PIZZA WITH QUICK CORNMEAL CRUST

Makes 6 servings

1¼ cups all-purpose flour
¾ cup plus 1 tablespoon yellow cornmeal
1½ tablespoons baking powder
¼ teaspoon ground cayenne pepper (optional)
¾ cup milk
2½ tablespoons vegetable oil
¾ pound lean ground beef
1 package (1.25 ounces) LAWRY'S® Taco Spices & Seasonings
¾ cup salsa
1 green bell pepper, sliced
1 medium tomato, sliced
2 cups (8 ounces) grated mozzarella cheese

In medium bowl, combine flour, ¾ cup cornmeal, baking powder and cayenne pepper. Add milk and oil; stir with fork until dough forms a ball. Sprinkle bottom of a lightly greased 15×10×1-inch jelly-roll pan or 14-inch round pan with remaining 1 tablespoon cornmeal. Press dough into pan. Bake in 425°F oven 12 to 15 minutes or until lightly browned. In medium skillet, brown ground beef, stirring until thoroughly cooked; drain fat. Add Taco Spices & Seasonings and salsa; blend well. Spread meat mixture over baked crust. Layer green pepper and tomato on top; sprinkle with cheese. Bake 15 minutes or until heated through and cheese is melted.

Presentation: Cut into squares or wedges. Serve with a tossed green salad.

COTTAGE PIZZA SUPREME

Makes 6 to 8 servings

1 package (13¾ ounces) hot roll mix
½ pound bulk Italian sausage, cooked and drained
2 cups Cottage cheese
1 can (12 ounces) seasoned tomato paste
1 cup (4 ounces) shredded Wisconsin Mozzarella cheese
½ cup chopped onion
½ pound mushrooms, sliced
½ cup (2 ounces) grated Wisconsin Parmesan cheese

Prepare roll mix according to package directions. Press onto bottom and sides of buttered 15×10-inch jelly-roll pan or 13-inch pizza pan. Let rise 30 minutes. Preheat oven to 375°F. Combine all remaining ingredients except Parmesan cheese in large bowl. Spread on prepared dough. Top with Parmesan cheese. Bake 35 minutes or until cheese is melted and bubbly.

Favorite recipe from **Wisconsin Milk Marketing Board © 1993**

Spicy Pizza with Quick Cornmeal Crust

CANADIAN-STYLE BACON PITA PIZZAS

Makes 4 servings
(2 pizzas per serving)

8 ounces Canadian-style bacon,
 cut into 1/8-inch-thick slices
6 teaspoons olive oil, divided
1 medium onion, cut into thin
 wedges
1/2 teaspoon dried oregano leaves,
 crushed
4 (6-inch) pita pocket breads,
 split horizontally
1/3 of 7-ounce jar roasted red
 peppers, cut into thin strips
1 cup (4 ounces) shredded
 Monterey Jack cheese with
 jalapeño peppers
1/4 cup sliced ripe olives

Preheat oven to 450°F. Cut
Canadian-style bacon into 1/2-inch
strips. Heat 2 teaspoons oil in small
skillet over medium-high heat until
hot. Add onion; cook and stir 3
minutes. Combine remaining 4
teaspoons oil and oregano in small
bowl. Place pita breads, smooth side
up, on baking sheets and brush
evenly with oregano mixture.
Top evenly with onion, bacon and
red peppers. Sprinkle cheese and
ripe olives evenly over tops. Bake 5
minutes or until cheese is melted.

Favorite recipe from **National Live Stock and
Meat Board**

Canadian-Style Bacon Pita Pizza

BAJA PIZZA POUCH
(Calzones)

Makes 8 calzones

1 pound bulk hot pork sausage
1/2 pound lean ground beef
1 can (12 ounces) refried beans
1 teaspoon ground cumin
1/4 teaspoon garlic powder
1 package (16 ounces) hot roll
 mix
1 can (14.5 ounces) crushed
 Italian flavored tomatoes
2 cups (8 ounces) shredded
 Wisconsin Monterey Jack
 cheese
1 cup (4 ounces) shredded
 Wisconsin Cheddar cheese
 Butter, melted
1 cup guacamole (optional)

Heat large skillet over medium heat
until hot. Crumble pork sausage and
ground beef into skillet. Cook,
stirring to separate meat, until no
pink remains. Drain off fat. Add
beans, cumin and garlic powder;
heat through.

Oil two baking sheets. Preheat oven to 400°F. Prepare hot roll mix according to package directions for pizza crust. Divide dough into eight pieces. Form each piece into a ball. On lightly floured surface, roll each ball into a 7-inch circle. Place dough circles on prepared baking sheets. Spread 1/2 cup meat mixture on 1/2 of each dough circle to within 1/2 inch of edge. Layer each calzone with 2 tablespoons crushed tomatoes, 1/4 cup Monterey Jack cheese and 2 tablespoons Cheddar cheese. Moisten edges of dough with water and fold over to enclose filling, pressing edges firmly together with fork. Brush with melted butter. Cut slit in each calzone to allow steam to escape. Bake 18 to 20 minutes or until golden brown. Serve with guacamole, if desired.

Favorite recipe from **Wisconsin Milk Marketing Board** © 1993

EASY BEEF TORTILLA PIZZAS

Makes 4 servings

- 1 **pound ground beef (80% lean)**
- 1 **medium onion, chopped**
- 1 **teaspoon dried oregano leaves, crushed**
- 1 **teaspoon salt**
- 4 **large (10-inch) flour tortillas**
- 4 **teaspoons olive oil**
- 1 **medium tomato, seeded and chopped**
  Greek Topping* *or* **Mexican Topping****

Preheat oven to 400°F. Heat large skillet over medium heat until hot. Crumble beef into skillet; add onion. Cook, stirring to separate meat, until no pink remains. Pour off drippings. Sprinkle oregano and salt over beef mixture, stirring to combine. Place tortillas on 2 large baking sheets. Lightly brush surface of each tortilla with oil. Bake tortillas 3 minutes. Spoon an equal portion of beef mixture evenly over top of each tortilla; evenly top with tomato and desired topping. Bake 12 to 14 minutes, rearranging baking sheets halfway through cooking time.

***Greek Topping:** 1 teaspoon dried basil leaves, crushed; 1/2 teaspoon lemon pepper; 4 ounces Feta cheese, crumbled; and 1/4 cup freshly grated Parmesan cheese.

****Mexican Topping:** 1 teaspoon dried cilantro (coriander) leaves, crushed; 1/2 teaspoon crushed dried red pepper; 1 cup shredded Monterey Jack or Cheddar cheese; and 1/3 cup sliced ripe olives.

Favorite recipe from **National Live Stock and Meat Board**

Easy Beef Tortilla Pizza

POULTRY PIZZAZZ

Looking for a new way to serve poultry? Sample Pesto Chicken Pizza, Turkey Pizza Pie, Chicken Parmesan Pizza or Turkey-Pepper Pizza and jazz up your next meal.

ROSEMARY CHICKEN SAUTÉ PIZZA

Makes 4 to 6 servings

2 half boneless chicken breasts, skinned and cut into strips
1 medium onion, sliced
½ teaspoon dried rosemary, crushed
1 tablespoon vegetable oil
1 (12-inch) prepared, pre-baked pizza crust*
1 can (14½ ounces) DEL MONTE® Pizza Style Chunky Tomatoes
2 cups shredded mozzarella cheese
1 green, yellow or red pepper, sliced

Preheat oven to 450°F. In large skillet, cook chicken, onion and rosemary in oil over medium-high heat; drain. Place crust on baking sheet. Spread tomatoes evenly over crust. Top with ½ of cheese, then chicken mixture, pepper slices and remaining cheese. Bake 10 minutes or until hot and bubbly.

Prep time: 10 minutes
Cook time: 10 minutes

TORTILLA FLATS

Makes 6 tortilla pizzas

1½ cups prepared pizza or spaghetti sauce
6 flour tortillas
1 cup thinly sliced mushrooms
6 to 8 slices turkey salami, cut into wedges
⅓ cup chopped green onion
1½ cups shredded Cheddar cheese

Preheat oven to 450°F. Spread ¼ cup sauce over each tortilla. Top each evenly with remaining ingredients. Bake 5 minutes or until cheese is melted. Cut into wedges.

Favorite recipe from **California Poultry Industry Federation**

Rosemary Chicken Sauté Pizza

44

Tortilla Flats (page 44) and Mexican Pizza Muffins

CHEESY FRANK PIZZA

Makes 8 servings

SAUCE
  1 tablespoon vegetable oil
  ¼ cup chopped onion
  1 can (14½ ounces) whole tomatoes
  1 can (8 ounces) tomato sauce
  1 bay leaf
  1 teaspoon sugar
  1 teaspoon dried oregano leaves, crushed
  Dash pepper

DOUGH
  1 package (¼ ounce) active dry yeast
  1 cup warm water (105° to 115°F), divided
  1 teaspoon salt
  2 tablespoons vegetable oil
  2½ to 3 cups all-purpose flour, divided

TOPPINGS
  Vegetable oil
  ½ cup grated Parmesan cheese
  1 cup sliced mushrooms
  1 (12-ounce) package turkey franks, thinly sliced
  2 cups (8 ounces) grated mozzarella cheese

To prepare sauce, heat 1 tablespoon oil in 3-quart saucepan. Add onion; cook and stir until onion is golden. Add tomatoes, breaking them up, tomato sauce, bay leaf, sugar, oregano and pepper. Bring to a boil. Reduce heat to low; simmer, covered, 30 minutes, stirring occasionally. Remove and discard bay leaf. Set aside to cool.

To prepare dough, dissolve yeast in ¼ cup warm water. Pour remaining ¾ cup warm water into large bowl. Add salt, 2 tablespoons oil and ½ cup flour. Stir in yeast mixture. Gradually add enough of remaining

MEXICAN PIZZA MUFFINS

Makes 2 servings

**4 turkey franks
8 Cheddar cheese slices
4 toasted English muffin halves
Salsa**

Preheat broiler. Slice franks, being careful not to cut all the way through, every ½ inch along length. Cook in simmering water until franks curl. Broil 2 slices of cheese on each toasted muffin half until cheese is melted; top each with curled frank and salsa.

Favorite recipe from **California Poultry Industry Federation**

flour to make smooth dough. Knead on well-floured surface 4 minutes. (Dough will be slightly sticky.) Lightly oil 15-inch pizza pan. Using oiled hands, spread dough over bottom and sides of pan; crimp edges to form rim. Let dough rise in warm place 15 to 20 minutes.

Preheat oven to 425°F. To assemble pizza, brush dough lightly with oil; spread reserved sauce over dough. Sprinkle with Parmesan cheese, mushrooms and franks. Top with mozzarella cheese. Bake 15 to 20 minutes or until crust is crisp and golden. Cut into wedges.

Favorite recipe from **California Poultry Industry Federation**

MEXICAN-STYLE PIZZAS

Makes 4 servings

- ½ **cup Basic Pizza Sauce (recipe follows)**
- ½ **cup hot or mild salsa**
- 1 **tablespoon minced cilantro or parsley**
- 4 **large flour tortillas**
- 1 **can (8 ounces) whole kernel corn, drained**
- 1 **can (5½ ounces) canned chicken or turkey, drained**
- ½ **cup drained canned pinto beans**
- 1 **can (4 ounces) green chilies, drained and cut into strips**
- 1 **cup (4 ounces) shredded Monterey Jack cheese**

Prepare Basic Pizza Sauce. Preheat broiler. Mix Basic Pizza Sauce, salsa and cilantro; spread on tortillas. Arrange corn, chicken, pinto beans and chilies over sauce; sprinkle with cheese. Broil 3 minutes or until cheese is melted.

Prep time: 10 minutes

Basic Pizza Sauce

- 1 **can (15 ounces) tomato puree**
- 1 **can (14½ ounces) whole tomatoes, drained and chopped**
- ½ **cup finely chopped onion**
- 1 **clove garlic, minced**
- ½ **teaspoon dried basil leaves, crushed**
- ¼ **teaspoon dried tarragon leaves, crushed**
- ¼ **teaspoon dried oregano leaves, crushed**

Combine all ingredients in large skillet; heat to boiling. Reduce heat and simmer 10 minutes. Cool.

Makes about 2½ cups

Tip: Basic Pizza Sauce can be prepared up to 3 days in advance; cover and refrigerate.

Hint: Use leftover sauce to prepare French-Style Pizzas (page 60) and Greek-Style Pizzas (page 29).

Prep time: 15 minutes

Favorite recipe from **Canned Food Information Council**

Clockwise from top left: Greek-Style Pizza (page 29), Mexican-Style Pizza and French-Style Pizza (page 60)

CHICKEN 'N' RICE PIZZA

Makes about 6 main-dish or 16 appetizer servings

    4 cups cooked rice
 ¹/₂ cup ground walnuts (optional)
    1 egg, beaten
 1¹/₂ cups (6 ounces) shredded Swiss
        cheese, divided
 ¹/₂ cup grated Parmesan cheese,
        divided
    2 tablespoons olive oil
    2 boneless, skinless chicken
        breast halves, cut into bite-
        size pieces
    1 small onion, sliced
 ¹/₂ green bell pepper, sliced
 ¹/₂ red bell pepper, sliced
 ¹/₄ pound fresh mushrooms, sliced
 ¹/₂ cup sliced pitted ripe olives
    1 jar (14 ounces) pizza sauce
    1 teaspoon dried basil leaves,
        crushed
    1 teaspoon dried oregano leaves,
        crushed
    1 cup (4 ounces) shredded
        mozzarella cheese

Preheat oven to 375°F. Combine rice, walnuts, if desired, egg, ¹/₂ cup Swiss cheese and ¹/₄ cup Parmesan cheese in large bowl. Press evenly over bottom and ¹/₂ inch up side of greased 14-inch pizza pan. Bake 10 minutes; set aside to cool.

Heat oil in large skillet over medium-high heat until hot. Add chicken, onion, peppers, mushrooms and olives. Cook and stir 7 minutes or until chicken is tender and no longer pink; drain off excess liquid.

Spread pizza sauce over cooled rice crust. Layer remaining 1 cup Swiss cheese, chicken mixture, basil and oregano over sauce. Top with mozzarella cheese and remaining ¹/₄ cup Parmesan cheese. Bake 15 to 20 minutes or until heated through. Let cool slightly before serving.

Chicken 'n' Rice Pizza

TURKEY PIZZA PIE

Makes 6 servings

    1 package (1¹/₂ ounces)
        spaghetti sauce mix
    1 can (6 ounces) tomato paste
        Water
    1 jar (2¹/₂ ounces) sliced
        mushrooms, drained
 ¹/₂ teaspoon dried oregano leaves,
        crushed
    1 pound ground turkey
 ¹/₄ cup milk
 ¹/₄ cup seasoned bread crumbs
    1 teaspoon garlic salt
 ¹/₄ teaspoon pepper
 ¹/₄ cup grated Parmesan cheese
    1 cup (4 ounces) shredded
        mozzarella cheese

Combine spaghetti sauce mix, tomato paste and ½ tomato paste can of water in medium saucepan. Add mushrooms and oregano. Bring to a boil; reduce heat. Simmer, uncovered, 10 minutes, stirring occasionally. Preheat oven to 350°F. Combine turkey, milk, bread crumbs, garlic salt and pepper in large bowl. Press turkey mixture evenly over bottom and sides of 9-inch pie plate. Spoon spaghetti sauce mixture evenly into meat crust. Sprinkle with Parmesan cheese. Bake 30 minutes. Sprinkle with mozzarella cheese. Bake 15 minutes longer. Cool slightly. Cut into wedges to serve.

Favorite recipe from **California Poultry Industry Federation**

PESTO CHICKEN PIZZA

Pesto Chicken Pizza

Makes 4 to 6 servings

1 **(12-inch) prepared, pre-baked pizza crust***
¼ **cup pesto sauce****
1 **can (14½ ounces) DEL MONTE® Pizza Style Chunky Tomatoes**
2 **cups shredded mozzarella cheese**
1½ **cups diced cooked chicken**
1 **small red or green pepper, thinly sliced**
1 **small zucchini, thinly sliced**
5 **medium mushrooms, thinly sliced**

Preheat oven to 450°F. Place crust on baking sheet. Spread pesto evenly over crust. Top with tomatoes, cheese and remaining ingredients. Bake 10 minutes or until hot and bubbly. Garnish with grated Parmesan cheese and chopped fresh basil, if desired.

*Substitute 4 (6-inch) prepared, pre-baked pizza crusts. Refrigerated or frozen pizza dough may also be used; prepare and bake according to package directions.

**Available frozen or refrigerated at the supermarket.

Prep time: 10 minutes
Cook time: 10 minutes

Helpful Hint: Toss vegetables in 1 tablespoon olive oil, if desired.

CHEESY TURKEY AND VEGETABLE PIZZA

Makes 1 (12-inch) pizza

- **1 can (10 ounces) refrigerated pizza crust**
- **¼ cup plus 1 tablespoon olive oil, divided**
- **1 jar (14 ounces) pizza sauce**
- **¾ pound boneless, skinless turkey breast tenderloin, cut into 1-inch cubes**
- **1 garlic clove, minced**
- **1 small onion, sliced into thin rings**
- **1 green bell pepper, sliced into thin rings**
- **½ pound fresh mushrooms, sliced**
- **1 can (2¼ ounces) sliced pitted ripe olives**
- **⅓ cup freshly grated Parmesan cheese**
- **1 teaspoon dried basil leaves, crushed**
- **1 cup (4 ounces) shredded Monterey Jack cheese**
- **1 cup (4 ounces) shredded Muenster cheese**

Preheat oven to 425°F. Unroll dough and press into greased 12-inch pizza pan or 13×9-inch pan. Brush 1 tablespoon oil evenly over dough, then spread with pizza sauce. Heat remaining ¼ cup oil in large skillet over medium-high heat until hot. Add turkey cubes and garlic; cook and stir 2 minutes. Add onion, green pepper and mushrooms; cook and stir 5 minutes longer or until turkey is tender and no longer pink. Spoon turkey mixture evenly over sauce. Top with olives. Sprinkle with Parmesan cheese and basil. Top with Monterey Jack and Muenster cheeses. Bake 20 minutes or until crust is golden brown.

CHICKEN PARMESAN PIZZA

Makes 4 to 6 servings

- **10 ounces chicken breasts, skinned, boned and cut into 1-inch slices**
- **¼ cup flour**
  Vegetable oil
- **2 cups tomato sauce, divided**
- **1 (12-inch) BOBOLI® Brand Italian Bread Shell**
- **¾ cup KRAFT® Natural Shredded Low-Moisture Part-Skim Mozzarella Cheese, divided**
- **8 black olives, pitted and halved**
- **1 tablespoon KRAFT® 100% Grated Parmesan Cheese**
- **½ teaspoon dried oregano leaves, crushed**

Dredge chicken in flour. Pour oil into large skillet 1 inch deep. Heat oil over medium-high heat until hot. Add chicken; fry until chicken is tender and golden brown. Remove to a paper towel with slotted spoon to absorb excess oil. Spread 1 cup tomato sauce over Boboli® Italian bread shell leaving 1-inch border. Sprinkle with ½ cup mozzarella cheese. Top with chicken, remaining 1 cup tomato sauce and olives. Sprinkle with remaining ¼ cup mozzarella cheese, Parmesan cheese and oregano. Bake on ungreased baking sheet in lower ⅓ of oven at 450°F about 8 to 10 minutes or until puffed and lightly browned.

Cheesy Turkey and Vegetable Pizza

Turkey-Pepper Pizza

uncovered, 4 minutes. Remove from heat. Pat and stretch bread dough into greased 15×10-inch jelly-roll pan. Spread turkey mixture evenly over dough. Top with onion and bell peppers. Sprinkle evenly with cheese. Bake in preheated oven at 400°F about 20 minutes or until golden brown. Cut into squares and serve with additional picante sauce.

TURKEY-PEPPER PIZZA

Makes 6 to 8 servings

1 tablespoon vegetable oil
1 garlic clove, minced
2 cups shredded or chopped cooked turkey
1 cup PACE® Picante Sauce
1 teaspoon dried oregano leaves, crushed
1 pound frozen bread dough, thawed
1 medium onion, thinly sliced and separated into rings
1 small green bell pepper, thinly sliced into rings or diced
1 small red bell pepper, thinly sliced into rings or diced
2 cups (8 ounces) shredded Monterey Jack or Cheddar cheese

Heat oil over medium-high heat in 10-inch skillet until hot. Add garlic; cook and stir 1 minute. Add turkey, picante sauce and oregano. Bring to a boil; reduce heat. Simmer,

EASY TURKEY PIZZA

Makes 6 servings

1 package (1.5 ounces) LAWRY'S® Extra Rich & Thick Spaghetti Sauce Spices & Seasonings
1 can (6 ounces) tomato paste
1¾ cups water
2 tablespoons IMPERIAL® Margarine
1 pound ground turkey
½ teaspoon LAWRY'S® Garlic Salt
½ teaspoon dried basil, crushed
¼ teaspoon LAWRY'S® Seasoned Pepper
1 large loaf (16 ounces) French bread, cut in half lengthwise
1 can (7 ounces) artichoke hearts, drained and chopped
1 medium onion, thinly sliced
2 cups (8 ounces) grated mozzarella cheese

In medium saucepan, prepare Extra Rich & Thick Spaghetti Sauce Spices & Seasonings with tomato paste, water and margarine according to package directions. In medium skillet, brown turkey; drain fat. Add Garlic Salt, basil and Seasoned Pepper. Place bread on baking sheet. Coat cut sides of bread with spaghetti sauce. Top each piece with ½ of turkey mixture, artichoke hearts, onion and cheese. Bake in 350°F oven 10 to 15 minutes or until cheese is melted and lightly browned.

Presentation: Serve with fruit salad.

Hint: For variety, more traditional pizza toppings may be added, such as pepperoni, olives, chopped green bell pepper or sliced mushrooms.

SAVORY MEXICAN POTATO PIZZA

Makes 4 to 6 servings

3 **medium russet potatoes (about 1 pound)**
 Water
½ **cup all-purpose flour**
¼ **cup cornmeal**
4 **tablespoons vegetable oil, divided**
½ **teaspoon garlic salt**
½ **teaspoon black pepper**
1 **jar (8 ounces) mild taco sauce**
1 **medium onion, chopped**
1 **cup shredded cooked chicken**
1 **cup (4 ounces) shredded Monterey Jack cheese**
1 **small jalapeño pepper, seeded and minced***
2 **tablespoons chopped fresh oregano**
 Prepared guacamole

Place potatoes in large saucepan; add enough water to cover. Bring to a boil over high heat. Reduce heat to low; cover and simmer 30 minutes or until potatoes are fork-tender. Drain; peel potatoes with paring knife when cool enough to handle. Mash potatoes with electric mixer at low speed.

Preheat oven to 350°F. Combine warm mashed potatoes, flour, cornmeal, 3 tablespoons oil, garlic salt and black pepper in large bowl; mix into smooth dough.

Dust hands lightly with flour. Press potato mixture onto bottom and up side of ungreased 10-inch tart pan with removable bottom. Combine taco sauce and onion in small bowl; spread evenly over potato mixture. Top with chicken, cheese and jalapeño. Sprinkle with oregano and remaining 1 tablespoon oil.

Bake 30 minutes or until potato mixture is heated through. Cool slightly, about 10 minutes. Carefully loosen pizza from rim of pan using table knife. Remove rim from pan. Remove pizza from pan bottom; cut into wedges. Serve with guacamole.

When working with jalapeño peppers, wear plastic disposable gloves and use caution to prevent irritation of skin or eyes.

Savory Mexican Potato Pizza

NEW WAVE SEAFOOD

Discover an array of innovative toppings with appetizing flavor combinations such as shrimp/jalapeño, salmon/caviar and clam/pesto. These creative pizzas are even perfect for entertaining.

INDIVIDUAL PIZZA

Makes 1 serving

- 1 (8-inch) flour tortilla
- ¼ cup spaghetti sauce or pizza sauce
- 1 can (3¼ ounces) STARKIST® Tuna, drained and broken into small chunks
- ¼ cup sliced mushrooms
- ¼ cup tomato slices
- 2 green or red bell pepper rings, cut into halves
- ¼ cup shredded low-fat Cheddar or mozzarella cheese

Preheat oven to 375°F. Place tortilla on a small baking sheet. Bake for 5 minutes, or until tortilla begins to crisp. Spread spaghetti sauce to within ½ inch of edge. Sprinkle tuna, mushrooms and tomato over tortilla. Arrange bell pepper half-rings on top. Sprinkle cheese over pizza. Bake for 8 to 10 minutes more, or until heated through.

Preparation time: 10 minutes

Tip: Flour tortillas make handy, low-calorie pizza "crusts" for individual pizzas.

NEW HAVEN WHITE PIZZA

Makes 2 to 4 servings

- 1 can (10 ounces) refrigerated pizza dough
- 2 tablespoons cornmeal
- 1 can (10 ounces) clams, drained
- 3 garlic cloves, minced
- 3 strips cooked bacon, crumbled
- 2 tablespoons Romano cheese
- 1 teaspoon dried oregano leaves, crushed
- ½ teaspoon TABASCO® Brand Pepper Sauce
  Olive oil

Preheat oven to 450°F. Prepare 12-inch round pizza crust according to package directions. Dust crust with cornmeal. Divide clams evenly over dough. Top evenly with garlic, bacon, Romano cheese and oregano. Drizzle with Tabasco® sauce and olive oil. Bake 15 minutes or until crust is golden brown.

Individual Pizza

Mother's Day Pizza Quiche

MOTHER'S DAY PIZZA QUICHE

Makes 1 (14-inch) pizza quiche

1 pound medium-size raw shrimp
¾ pound skinless, boneless chicken breasts
2 tablespoons corn oil
½ pound mushrooms, sliced
1 large onion, sliced
1 small green pepper, cut into julienne strips
2 cans (10 ounces each) refrigerated pizza dough
4 ounces SAGA® Garlic/Chive Cheese, broken into small pieces
3 eggs
1½ cups half-and-half
Toasted sesame seeds
3 green onions, sliced

Place shrimp and chicken in large saucepan; cover with water. Bring to a boil; lower heat and simmer, covered, 10 minutes. Drain and cool. Dice chicken. Set aside 8 shrimp for garnish.

Heat oil in large skillet over medium heat until hot. Add mushrooms, onion and green pepper; cook and stir 5 minutes or until onion is soft. Cool.

Preheat oven to 400°F. Unroll pizza dough. Place 1 piece on top of the other. Roll out on lightly floured surface to 15-inch square. Trim corners to make a 15-inch round, reserving scraps for garnish. Place dough in lightly oiled 14-inch pizza pan. Turn under edges; crimp edges to form rim. Spread mushroom mixture evenly over dough and sprinkle with shrimp, chicken and cheese. Beat eggs in small bowl; reserve 1 tablespoon for glazing. Beat half-and-half into eggs. Pour mixture evenly over pizza.

Bake 25 to 30 minutes or until puffed and brown. Cut 4 hearts from scraps of pizza dough. Shape scraps of dough into 3 letters: M-O-M, if desired. Place dough hearts and letters on baking sheet; brush with reserved beaten egg. Sprinkle with sesame seeds. Bake with pizza quiche for 5 to 6 minutes or until golden brown. Decorate edge of pizza with reserved shrimp and green onions. Arrange hearts and letters in center.

Favorite recipe from **Tholstrup Cheese U.S.A., Inc.**

SEAFOOD PIZZA SUPREME

Makes 1 (15-inch) pizza

8 ounces peeled, cooked small shrimp, crabmeat or crab-flavored surimi seafood product (or combination of all three)

7½ teaspoons olive oil, divided

¾ teaspoon dried oregano leaves, crushed and divided

1 cup sliced mushrooms

⅛ teaspoon freshly ground black pepper

1 loaf (1 pound) frozen bread dough, thawed overnight in refrigerator and warmed at room temperature 1 hour
Cornmeal
Dash crushed dried red pepper

1 cup (4 ounces) shredded mozzarella cheese, divided

3 tablespoons grated Parmesan cheese

Preheat oven to 425°F. Combine seafood with 3 teaspoons oil and ¼ teaspoon oregano. Combine mushrooms, black pepper, remaining 4½ teaspoons oil and ½ teaspoon oregano. Knead dough lightly to remove air bubbles. Roll out into 16-inch circle. Sprinkle 15-inch pizza pan or large baking sheet with cornmeal. Press dough circle into pan; crimp edges to form rim. Sprinkle with red pepper and ½ cup mozzarella cheese; top with mushroom mixture. Sprinkle with remaining ½ cup mozzarella cheese. Bake 10 minutes or until crust is lightly browned. Remove from oven. Arrange seafood on pizza. Sprinkle with Parmesan cheese. Bake 3 to 5 minutes longer or until thoroughly heated.

Favorite recipe from **National Fisheries Institute**

TOM TOMPKIN'S SMOKED SALMON PIZZA

Makes 4 (6-inch) pizzas

2 bunches fresh dill

2 packages (8 ounces each) cream cheese, softened

2 bunches fresh chives, thinly sliced

4 (6-inch) Italian bread shells

8 ounces smoked salmon, cut into ¼-inch strips

2 teaspoons red lumpfish caviar

2 teaspoons black lumpfish caviar

2 teaspoons gold lumpfish caviar

2 teaspoons salmon caviar

Preheat oven to 350°F. Reserve 20 sprigs of dill for garnish. Chop remaining dill. Mix cream cheese, chives and chopped dill in small bowl until smooth.

Heat bread shells on ungreased baking sheet 3 to 4 minutes or until shells are crisp. Spread herbed cheese mixture generously on shells. Sprinkle smoked salmon onto herbed cheese mixture. Randomly sprinkle all caviars and dill sprigs over pizzas.

Favorite recipe from **National Fisheries Institute**

Seafood Pizza Supreme

JAMBALAYA PIZZA

Makes 4 to 6 servings

- **1 pound sausage, cut into 1-inch pieces**
- **1 teaspoon olive oil**
- **2 cups cubed OSCAR MAYER® Ham**
- **³/₄ cup thinly sliced green pepper**
- **¹/₃ cup sliced onion**
- **¹/₄ cup diced celery**
- **1 cup canned tomatoes, drained and coarsely chopped**
- **¹/₂ pound raw large shrimp, shelled and deveined**
- **1 teaspoon dried thyme leaves, crushed**
- **¹/₂ teaspoon pepper sauce**
- **1 (12-inch) BOBOLI® Brand Italian Bread Shell**
- **1 tablespoon chopped parsley**

Cook sausage in large skillet until it loses pink color. Drain fat. Remove sausage with slotted spoon. Heat oil over medium-high heat in same skillet until hot. Add ham, green pepper, onion and celery; cook and stir until slightly seared. Reduce heat to medium-low. Add tomatoes, reserved sausage, shrimp, thyme and pepper sauce; simmer uncovered until most of liquid is evaporated and shrimp are opaque. Salt and pepper to taste. Fill Boboli® Italian bread shell leaving a 1-inch border. Bake on ungreased baking sheet in lower ¹/₃ of oven at 450°F about 8 to 10 minutes or until puffed and lightly browned. Sprinkle with parsley and serve.

EASY CALZONE

Makes 4 servings

- **1 can (10 ounces) refrigerated ready-to-use pizza dough**
- **1 package (10 ounces) frozen chopped spinach, thawed**
- **1 can (9¹/₄ ounces) STARKIST® Tuna, drained and flaked**
- **1 cup chopped tomatoes**
- **2 cans (4 ounces each) sliced mushrooms, drained**
- **1 cup shredded low-fat Cheddar or mozzarella cheese**
- **1 teaspoon Italian seasoning or dried oregano, crushed**
- **1 teaspoon dried basil, crushed**
- **¹/₄ teaspoon garlic powder**
  Vegetable oil
  Cornmeal (optional)
- **1 can (8 ounces) pizza sauce**

Preheat oven to 425°F. Unroll pizza dough onto a lightly floured board; cut crosswise into 2 equal pieces. Roll each piece of dough into a 12-inch circle.

Squeeze all liquid from spinach; chop fine. Over the bottom half of each circle of dough, sprinkle spinach, tuna, tomatoes, mushrooms, cheese and seasonings to within 1 inch of bottom edge. Fold top half of dough over filling, leaving bottom edge uncovered. Moisten bottom edge of dough with a little water, then fold bottom edge of dough over top edge, sealing with fingers or crimping with fork. Brush top of dough lightly with oil; sprinkle with cornmeal if desired. Place 2 filled calzones on ungreased baking sheet; bake for 25 to 30 minutes, or until deep golden brown. Meanwhile, in saucepan, heat pizza sauce. Cut each calzone in half crosswise to serve. Pass sauce to spoon over.

Preparation time: 25 minutes

Note: "Calzone" is Italian for a filled turnover made with pizza dough.

Easy Calzone

CLAM AND PESTO PIZZA

Makes 1 (15-inch) pizza

1 loaf (1 pound) frozen bread dough, thawed overnight in refrigerator and warmed at room temperature 1 to 2 hours
Cornmeal
1 tablespoon olive oil
1 clove garlic, minced
1 (10-ounce) or 2 (6½-ounce) cans chopped clams, well drained *or* 2 pounds fresh medium clams, steamed and chopped *or* 1¼ pounds mussels in the shell, steamed and chopped (steaming directions follow)
¼ cup Processor Pesto Sauce* (recipe follows)
¾ cup shredded Monterey Jack or mozzarella cheese
2 tablespoons thinly sliced green onions
2 tablespoons minced fresh parsley
¼ cup grated Parmesan cheese

Preheat oven to 425°F. Knead dough lightly to remove air bubbles. Roll out dough to 15-inch circle. Sprinkle 15-inch pizza pan or large baking sheet with cornmeal. Press dough into prepared pan. Crimp edges to form rim. Combine oil and garlic. Brush ½ of garlic mixture over dough; toss clams or mussels with remaining garlic mixture. Bake dough 10 minutes or until lightly brown. Spread crust with Processor Pesto Sauce; sprinkle with Monterey Jack cheese. Top with clam or mussel mixture, then green onions and parsley. Sprinkle with Parmesan cheese. Bake 3 to 5 minutes longer or until seafood is thoroughly heated.

Steaming Directions: Scrub clams or mussels with stiff brush under cold running water; rinse well. Discard any that do not close when tapped. Debeard mussels. Place in large, heavy saucepan and add ½ cup boiling water. Cover and steam over medium-high heat until shells open, about 4 minutes for clams, 2 minutes for mussels. Discard any with unopened shells. Drain liquid; cool slightly. Remove meat from shells; chop. Refrigerate until needed.

Processor Pesto Sauce: Combine 2 cups lightly packed fresh basil leaves, ¼ cup parsley sprigs, ¼ cup pine nuts (optional), ⅓ cup olive oil, 1 peeled garlic clove and ⅛ teaspoon salt in bowl of food processor. Process until smooth. Refrigerate or freeze extra sauce.

Makes about ⅔ cup

*Prepared pesto sauce, available in the deli section, may be substituted.

Favorite recipe from **National Fisheries Institute**

FRENCH-STYLE PIZZAS

Makes 4 servings

1 cup Basic Pizza Sauce (page 47)
¼ teaspoon dried tarragon leaves, crushed
⅛ teaspoon dried thyme leaves, crushed
4 pita bread rounds
1 can (10 ounces) baby or minced clams, drained
1 can (4¼ ounces) medium shrimp, rinsed and drained
1 small red bell pepper, sliced
8 pitted ripe olives, sliced
1 tablespoon drained capers
¼ cup crumbled goat cheese

Prepare Basic Pizza Sauce. Preheat broiler. Mix Basic Pizza Sauce, tarragon and thyme; spread on pita bread rounds. Arrange clams, shrimp, red pepper and olives over sauce. Sprinkle with capers and goat cheese. Broil until cheese is melted.

Prep time: 10 minutes

Favorite recipe from **Canned Food Information Council**

NORTH SEA SARDINE RAFTS

Makes 6 servings

1 package (10 ounces) frozen pastry shells, thawed*
1³/₄ cups shredded Nokkelost cheese
6 thin slices yellow onion, separated into rings
2 cans (3³/₄ ounces each) Norwegian sardines in oil, drained
1¹/₂ tablespoons olive oil

Preheat oven to 400°F. Roll out 3 pastry shells on each of two ungreased baking sheets into 6- to 7-inch rounds. Prick with tines of fork. Bake about 4 minutes or just until very lightly browned around edges. Remove from oven. (Pastry will puff slightly and may look undone.)

Sprinkle about ¹/₂ of cheese on baked pastries. Top each with onion rings and 4 sardines. Drizzle with olive oil. Sprinkle with remaining cheese. Bake 6 minutes or until heated through and cheese is melted.

Salmon Rafts: Prepare pastries as above. Substitute 1¹/₄ cups canned salmon for the sardines. Sprinkle lightly with dried dill weed. Drizzle with oil and cheese; bake as above.

*Thaw unopened in refrigerator. They should be dry and slightly firm to the touch—not soft and damp.

Favorite recipe from **Norseland Foods, Inc.**

Seafood Topped Mexican Pizzas

SEAFOOD TOPPED MEXICAN PIZZAS

Makes 12 individual pizzas

¹/₂ cup canned enchilada sauce
12 (6-inch) corn tortillas
1 cup shredded Cheddar cheese
8 ounces crab-flavored surimi seafood, tiny cooked shrimp, crabmeat or a combination of all three
1 can (2¹/₄ ounces) sliced ripe olives, drained
¹/₄ cup seeded and sliced jalapeño peppers*
1 cup (4 ounces) shredded Monterey Jack cheese

Preheat oven to 400°F. Spread enchilada sauce on tortillas; sprinkle with Cheddar cheese. Place on ungreased baking sheets; bake 5 minutes. Remove from oven. Arrange seafood, olives and peppers on pizzas and sprinkle with Monterey Jack cheese. Bake 3 minutes longer or just until seafood is hot and cheese is melted. Serve with hot pepper sauce, if desired.

*When working with jalapeño peppers, wear plastic disposable gloves and use caution to prevent irritation of skin or eyes.

Favorite recipe from **National Fisheries Institute**

JUST VEGGIES

What a delectable way to get your veggies! You'll find Cheesy Asparagus Pizza, Marinated Bell Pepper & Mushroom Pizza, Calzone Italiano and Plum Tomato Basil Pizza to inspire meatless meals.

FAST-PACED BLACK BEAN PIZZA

Makes 6 to 8 servings

1 medium onion, chopped
2 cloves garlic, minced
1 tablespoon olive oil
¾ cup PACE® Picante Sauce
1 can (16 ounces) black beans, rinsed and drained
1 teaspoon ground cumin
½ teaspoon dried basil leaves, crushed (optional)
1 (12-inch) prepared pizza crust
1 large red or green bell pepper, sliced into thin rings
1½ cups (6 ounces) shredded Monterey Jack cheese
Grated Parmesan cheese (optional)

Cook onion and garlic in oil in 10-inch skillet, stirring occasionally, until tender, about 4 minutes. Stir in picante sauce, beans, cumin and basil, if desired. Simmer 2 minutes. Spread evenly over crust. Overlap pepper rings over bean mixture. Sprinkle with Monterey Jack cheese. Bake in preheated oven at 425°F. 15 minutes or until cheese is bubbly.

Cut into wedges to serve. Serve with additional picante sauce and Parmesan cheese, if desired.

TACO PIZZA

Makes 6 (7-inch) pizzas

6 (7-inch) flour tortillas
1 can (16 ounces) refried beans
¾ teaspoon ground cumin
1 can (14½ ounces) DEL MONTE® Pizza Style Chunky Tomatoes
2 cups shredded sharp Cheddar or Monterey Jack cheese
1½ cups shredded lettuce
½ cup sour cream

Preheat oven to 450°F. Place tortillas on baking sheet. Spread beans evenly over tortillas. Stir cumin into tomatoes. Spread over beans. Top with cheese. Bake 6 to 8 minutes or until hot and bubbly. Serve with lettuce and sour cream.

Prep time: 5 minutes
Cook time: 8 minutes

Fast-Paced Black Bean Pizza

GREEK PIZZA

Makes 1 main-dish or
2 appetizer servings

1 **pita bread, cut in half**
   Olive oil
¼ **cup CONTADINA® Pizza**
   Squeeze Pizza Sauce, divided
1 **tablespoon chopped Greek**
   olives
1 **tablespoon crumbled feta**
   cheese
1 **tablespoon shredded**
   mozzarella cheese
2 **teaspoons chopped green onion**

Brush pita halves lightly with oil;
bake on baking sheet in preheated
425°F. oven for 5 minutes. Spread
with pizza sauce; sprinkle with
olives, feta cheese, mozzarella
cheese and green onion. Bake at
425°F. for 5 minutes or until cheese
is melted.

Clockwise from top right: Kona Coast Pizza (page 9),
Quesadilla Pizza (page 7) and Greek Pizza

SPUNKY VEGETABLE PIZZA

Makes 4 servings

¾ **cup pizza sauce**
1 **large pizza shell**
1 **cup chopped DOLE® Broccoli**
1 **cup shredded DOLE® Carrots**
½ **cup sliced DOLE® Red or Green**
   Bell Pepper
5 **to 6 ounces shredded low-fat**
   mozzarella cheese

• Spoon pizza sauce on pizza shell.
Place on cookie sheet.

• Arrange vegetables over sauce.

• Sprinkle with cheese.

• Bake in 450°F oven 10 minutes.

• Cut into 8 wedges.

Prep time: 15 minutes
Bake time: 10 minutes

GARDEN STYLE PIZZA

Makes 8 servings

1 cup QUAKER® Oats (quick or
   old fashioned, uncooked)
1¼ cups all-purpose flour
1 teaspoon baking powder
½ teaspoon salt (optional)
¾ cup skim milk
2 tablespoons vegetable oil
2 cups sliced mushrooms
1½ cups shredded carrots
1 cup thinly sliced zucchini
½ cup chopped onion
1 teaspoon vegetable oil
1 (8-ounce) can pizza sauce
1½ cups (6 ounces) shredded part-
   skim mozzarella cheese
½ teaspoon Italian seasoning
   (optional)

Heat oven to 425°F. Spray 12-inch round pizza pan with vegetable oil cooking spray or oil lightly. Place oats in blender container or food processor bowl; cover. Blend about 1 minute, stopping occasionally to stir. Combine ground oats, flour, baking powder and salt. Add milk and 2 tablespoons oil; stir with fork until mixture forms a ball. Knead dough on lightly floured surface about 10 times. With greased fingers, press dough into prepared pan; shape edge to form rim. Bake 20 minutes or until light golden brown.

Saute mushrooms, carrots, zucchini and onion in 1 teaspoon oil over low heat about 3 minutes. Spoon pizza sauce over partially baked crust, spreading evenly to edge; top with sauteed vegetables. Sprinkle with cheese and Italian seasoning; continue baking about 15 minutes or until cheese is melted.

SPINACH & CHEESE STROMBOLI

Makes 2 loaves, about 8 slices each

¼ cup plus 2 tablespoons
   WISH-BONE® Italian or
   Robusto Italian Dressing
1 cup sliced mushrooms
½ cup sliced onion
½ cup chopped red or green bell
   pepper
1 package (10 ounces) frozen
   chopped spinach, cooked and
   squeezed dry
½ cup grated Parmesan cheese
⅛ teaspoon black pepper
2 loaves (1 pound each) frozen
   bread dough, thawed
1 package (8 ounces) mozzarella
   cheese, shredded
1 egg, slightly beaten

Preheat oven to 375°F.

In large skillet, heat ¼ cup Italian dressing and cook mushrooms, onion and red pepper over medium-high heat, stirring occasionally, 15 minutes or until tender. Stir in spinach, Parmesan cheese and black pepper.

On lightly floured board, roll each bread loaf into a 10×7-inch rectangle. Sprinkle ½ of mozzarella cheese, then spread ½ of spinach mixture over each rectangle, leaving ½-inch border. Roll, starting at long end, jelly-roll style; pinch ends to seal. Place rolls seam-side down on lightly greased baking sheet, then brush lightly with remaining 2 tablespoons Italian dressing beaten with egg. Bake 45 minutes or until golden. Slice and serve warm.

MEDITERRANEAN VEGETABLE PIZZA

Makes 4 servings

1 (6.5-ounce) package ALOUETTE LIGHT® Spring Vegetable cheese
4 (6-inch) pita bread rounds
2 tablespoons olive oil
1 Spanish onion, thinly sliced
4 Italian plum tomatoes, diced
1/3 cup sliced pitted black olives
1/4 cup julienned basil leaves
   Freshly ground black pepper

Preheat oven to 400°F. Spread 3 tablespoons cheese evenly on top of each pita round. Heat oil over medium heat in 10-inch skillet until hot. Add onion; cook and stir 3 to 4 minutes or until golden. Add tomatoes and olives; cook and stir 1 1/2 to 2 minutes longer or until no liquid remains. Top each pita with vegetable mixture, basil and pepper; bake 5 to 6 minutes. Cut into wedges; serve immediately.

Favorite recipe from **Bongrain Cheese U.S.A.**

PIZZA MARGHERITA

Makes 4 servings

3/4 cup shredded mozzarella cheese
1/2 cup shredded Swiss cheese
3 tablespoons grated Parmesan cheese
2 cloves garlic, minced
1 tablespoon olive oil
4 (6-inch) prepared, pre-baked pizza crusts* *or* 4 (7-inch) pita pocket breads
1 can (14 1/2 ounces) DEL MONTE® Pizza Style Chunky Tomatoes
1/4 cup thinly sliced fresh basil leaves *or* 1 teaspoon dried basil, crushed

Preheat oven to 450°F. In bowl, toss cheeses together; set aside. In small pan, cook garlic in oil over low heat 2 minutes. Place crusts on baking sheet. Spread garlic mixture evenly over crusts. Top with tomatoes, 1/2 of cheese and basil. Top with remaining cheese. Bake 6 to 8 minutes or until hot and bubbly.

Substitute 1 large pizza crust for 4 small crusts. Bake 10 to 14 minutes or until hot and bubbly.

Prep time: 12 minutes
Cook time: 8 minutes

SICILIAN PIZZA

Makes 4 to 6 servings

2 onions, sliced
2 cloves garlic, minced
2 tablespoons oil
1 (12-inch) prepared, pre-baked pizza crust*
1 can (14 1/2 ounces) DEL MONTE® Pizza Style Chunky Tomatoes
2 cups shredded mozzarella cheese
2 tablespoons grated Parmesan cheese

Preheat oven to 450°F. In skillet, cook onions and garlic in oil until soft. Place pizza crust on baking sheet. Spread tomatoes evenly over crust. Top with mozzarella cheese, onion mixture and Parmesan cheese. Bake 10 minutes or until hot and bubbly.

Substitute 4 (6-inch) prepared, pre-baked pizza crusts. Refrigerated or frozen pizza dough may also be used; prepare and bake according to package directions.

Prep time: 15 minutes
Cook time: 15 minutes

PIZZA WITH FONTINA, ARTICHOKE HEARTS AND RED ONION

Makes 4 servings

1 pound frozen white bread dough, thawed according to package directions
2 tablespoons olive oil, divided
2 tablespoons wheat bran
1 large clove garlic, chopped finely
½ medium red onion, thinly sliced
1 package (9 ounces) frozen artichoke hearts, thawed *or* 1 can (14 ounces) artichoke hearts, drained and sliced lengthwise
Salt
Freshly ground black pepper
1 cup (4 ounces) shredded Wisconsin Fontina cheese

Preheat oven to 450°F. On lightly oiled baking sheet, press chilled dough into 12×9-inch rectangle; crimp edges to form rim. Brush with 1 tablespoon oil. Evenly sprinkle with bran; press lightly into dough. Sprinkle with garlic. Arrange onion in 1 layer over dough; top with artichoke hearts. Drizzle with remaining 1 tablespoon oil. Lightly season with salt and pepper. Evenly sprinkle with cheese. (Do not let dough rise. The pizza may be held briefly in the refrigerator before baking.) Bake 15 minutes or until crust is golden brown.

Favorite recipe from **Wisconsin Milk Marketing Board** © 1993

Pizza with Fontina, Artichoke Hearts and Red Onion

CALZONE ITALIANO

Makes 4 servings

1 loaf frozen bread dough, thawed*
1 can (15 ounces) DEL MONTE® Chopped Spinach
8 ounces ricotta cheese
1 can (14½ ounces) DEL MONTE Pizza Style Chunky Tomatoes
1½ cups shredded mozzarella cheese

Preheat oven to 400°F. Divide dough into four portions. On floured board, roll dough into 7-inch rounds. Drain spinach, squeezing out excess liquid. Spread half of each round with ricotta cheese, tomatoes, spinach and mozzarella cheese. Fold each round in half, folding dough over filling; pinch edges to seal. Place on baking sheet. Brush with olive oil, if desired. Bake 15 to 20 minutes or until golden.

Refrigerated pizza dough may be used; prepare according to package directions.

Prep time: 15 minutes
Cook time: 20 minutes

VEGETABLE PIZZA WITH OAT BRAN CRUST

Makes 4 servings

- 1 cup QUAKER® Oat Bran™ Hot Cereal, uncooked
- 1 cup all-purpose flour
- 1 teaspoon baking powder
- ¾ cup skim milk
- 3 tablespoons vegetable oil
- 1 tablespoon QUAKER® Oat Bran™ Hot Cereal, uncooked
- 1 can (8 ounces) low sodium tomato sauce
- 1 cup sliced mushrooms (about 3 ounces)
- 1 medium green, red or yellow bell pepper or combination, cut into rings
- ½ cup chopped onion
- 1¼ cups (5 ounces) shredded part skim mozzarella cheese
- ½ teaspoon oregano leaves or Italian seasoning, crushed

Combine 1 cup oat bran, flour and baking powder. Add milk and oil; mix well. Let stand 10 minutes.

Heat oven to 425°F. Lightly spray 12-inch round pizza pan with vegetable oil cooking spray or oil lightly. Sprinkle with 1 tablespoon oat bran. With lightly oiled fingers, pat dough out evenly; shape edge to form rim. Bake 18 to 20 minutes. Spread sauce evenly over partially baked crust. Top with vegetables; sprinkle with cheese and oregano. Bake an additional 12 to 15 minutes or until golden brown. Cut into 8 wedges.

VEGETABLE CALZONE

Makes 4 servings

- 1 loaf (1 pound) frozen bread dough
- 1 package (10 ounces) frozen chopped broccoli, thawed and well drained
- 1 cup (8 ounces) SARGENTO® Light Ricotta Cheese
- 1 cup (4 ounces) SARGENTO® Classic Supreme™ Shredded Mozzarella Cheese
- 1 clove garlic, minced
- ¼ teaspoon white pepper
- 1 egg beaten with 1 tablespoon water
- 1 jar (16 ounces) spaghetti sauce, heated (optional)
- SARGENTO® Grated Parmesan Cheese (optional)

Thaw bread dough and let rise according to package directions. Combine broccoli, Ricotta and Mozzarella cheeses, garlic and pepper. Punch down bread dough and turn out onto lightly floured surface. Divide into 4 equal pieces. One at a time, roll out each piece into an 8-inch circle. Place about ¾ cup cheese mixture on half of the circle, leaving a 1-inch border. Fold dough over to cover filling, forming a semi-circle; press and crimp the edges with fork tines to seal. Brush with egg mixture. Place on greased baking sheet and bake at 350°F 30 minutes or until brown and puffed. Transfer to rack and let cool 10 minutes. Top with hot spaghetti sauce and Parmesan cheese.

Vegetable Pizza with Oat Bran Crust

Peanut Butter Pizza

PEANUT BUTTER PIZZA

Makes 2 (12-inch) pizzas

- 1 **cup warm water (105° to 115°F)**
- 1 **package (¼ ounce) active dry yeast**
- 1 **teaspoon sugar**
- 1½ **teaspoons salt, divided**
- 4 **tablespoons peanut oil, divided**
- 3 to 3¼ **cups unsifted flour**
- 1 **cup chopped green bell pepper**
- ⅔ **cup chopped onion**
- 2 **cloves garlic, finely chopped**
- 2 **cups tomato sauce**
- ½ **teaspoon dried oregano leaves, crushed**
- ½ **teaspoon dried basil leaves, crushed**
- ½ **teaspoon chili powder**
- ¼ **teaspoon black pepper**
- 3 **cups grated Cheddar cheese**
- ½ **cup peanut butter**
- 3 **slices mozzarella cheese, cut in half to form triangles**

Place warm water in large warm bowl. Sprinkle yeast over water. Stir until dissolved. Add sugar, 1 teaspoon salt, 2 tablespoons peanut oil and 1½ cups flour. Beat until smooth. Stir in enough of remaining flour to form a soft dough. Turn out onto lightly floured board and knead* 8 to 10 minutes or until smooth and elastic. Place in greased bowl, turning to grease top. Cover; let rise in warm draft-free place 45 minutes or until double in bulk.

Meanwhile, place green pepper, onion, garlic and remaining 2 tablespoons peanut oil in top of double boiler. Place over simmering water; cook until vegetables are tender. Add tomato sauce, oregano, basil, chili powder, remaining ½ teaspoon salt and black pepper. Cover double boiler; cook over low heat 10 minutes, stirring occasionally. Add Cheddar cheese and peanut butter. Cook over simmering water until cheese is melted and mixture is blended.

Preheat oven to 400°F. Punch dough down. Divide in half. On lightly floured surface, roll each half into 13-inch circle. Place each circle in greased 12-inch pizza pan; crimp edges to form rim. Spread tomato sauce mixture on dough. Place mozzarella triangles as desired; bake 25 minutes or until crust is golden brown.

To knead dough, fold in half toward you and press dough away from you with heels of hands. Give dough a quarter turn and continue folding, pushing and turning.

Favorite recipe from **Oklahoma Peanut Commission**

THICK 'N CHEESY VEGETABLE PIZZA

Makes about 6 servings

2 loaves (1 pound each) frozen bread dough, thawed
1 envelope LIPTON® Recipe Secrets Vegetable Recipe Soup Mix
¼ cup olive or vegetable oil
2 tablespoons chopped fresh basil leaves*
1 large clove garlic, finely chopped
¼ teaspoon pepper
2 cups shredded mozzarella cheese
1 cup fresh or canned sliced mushrooms
1 medium tomato, coarsely chopped

Preheat oven to 425°F.

Into lightly oiled 12-inch pizza pan, press dough to form crust; set aside.

In small bowl, blend vegetable recipe soup mix, oil, basil, garlic and pepper; spread evenly on dough. Top with remaining ingredients. Bake 20 minutes or until cheese is melted and crust is golden brown. To serve, cut into wedges.

Substitution: Use 2 teaspoons dried basil leaves.

MINI VEGETABLE PIZZA

Makes 6 servings

6 English muffins
⅓ cup olive oil
3 tablespoons FRENCH'S® CLASSIC YELLOW® Mustard
¼ teaspoon paprika
¼ teaspoon garlic powder
3 cups assorted cut-up vegetables (carrots, green onion, broccoli and/or red bell pepper)
1½ cups (6 ounces) shredded mozzarella cheese
2 tablespoons (1 ounce) grated Parmesan cheese

Separate English muffins and place on 15×10-inch baking sheet. In small bowl combine oil, mustard, paprika and garlic powder. Spread about 2 teaspoons on each muffin half. Bake at 400°F for 10 minutes. Top each muffin with vegetables and cheeses, dividing evenly. Bake for 5 minutes or until cheese is melted.

Thick 'n Cheesy Vegetable Pizza

Top to bottom: Plum Tomato Basil Pizza and New Haven White Pizza (page 54)

THREE CHEESE PIZZA

Makes 4 servings

4 (6-inch) prepared, pre-baked pizza crusts *or* 4 (6-inch) pita pocket breads
1 can (14½ ounces) DEL MONTE® Pizza Style Chunky Tomatoes
¾ cup shredded mozzarella cheese
½ cup shredded Swiss cheese
3 tablespoons grated Parmesan cheese

Preheat oven to 450°F. Place crusts on baking sheet. Spread tomatoes evenly over crusts. Top with cheeses. Bake 6 to 8 minutes or until hot and bubbly.

Prep time: 12 minutes
Cook time: 8 minutes

Variation: Substitute 8 toasted English muffin halves for pizza crusts.

PLUM TOMATO BASIL PIZZA

Makes 2 to 4 servings

1 can (10 ounces) refrigerated pizza dough
2 tablespoons cornmeal
1 cup (8 ounces) shredded mozzarella cheese
4 ripe, seeded Italian plum tomatoes, sliced
½ cup fresh basil leaves
½ teaspoon TABASCO® Brand Pepper Sauce
Olive oil

Preheat oven to 425°F. Prepare 12-inch round pizza crust according to package directions. Dust crust with cornmeal. Sprinkle mozzarella cheese evenly over crust. Layer with tomato slices and basil leaves. Drizzle with Tabasco® sauce and olive oil. Bake for 15 minutes or until crust is golden brown.

BEANIZZA

Makes 4 servings
(2 wedges per serving)

Nonstick cooking spray
1 small zucchini, sliced (about 1 cup)
½ cup sliced fresh mushrooms
½ cup sliced green onions
½ teaspoon Italian seasoning
1 can (16 ounces) HEINZ® Vegetarian Beans in Tomato Sauce
2 tablespoons grated Parmesan cheese
1 pre-baked pizza shell (12-inch)
1 cup shredded mozzarella cheese
½ cup finely shredded Cheddar cheese

Spray large skillet with cooking spray. Sauté zucchini, mushrooms, green onions and Italian seasoning until vegetables are tender-crisp. Stir in beans and Parmesan cheese. Simmer 5 minutes, stirring occasionally. Place pizza shell on cookie sheet. Spoon vegetable mixture evenly over pizza shell; sprinkle mozzarella cheese on top. Bake in preheated 425°F oven, 10 to 12 minutes or until shell is lightly browned. Remove from oven and sprinkle with Cheddar cheese; cut into 8 wedges.

GRILLED VEGETABLES PIZZA

Makes 4 to 6 servings

1 teaspoon salt
2 cups (1/4-inch) zucchini slices
10 (1/4-inch) eggplant slices
2 tablespoons olive oil
1 (12-inch) BOBOLI® Brand Italian Bread Shell
1 cup KRAFT® Natural Shredded Low-Moisture Part-Skim Mozzarella Cheese, divided
1/4 cup (1/4-inch) roasted red pepper slices
1 tablespoon coarsely chopped fresh basil leaves

Preheat grill. Lightly salt zucchini and eggplant. Brush with oil. Grill on both sides until tender. Sprinkle Boboli® Italian bread shell with 1/2 cup cheese. Top with grilled vegetables, roasted red peppers, basil and remaining 1/2 cup cheese. Place bread shell on grill 5 inches from coals. Cover and grill for 3 to 4 minutes or until cheese is melted.

GOURMET SOUTHERN PIZZA

Makes 4 to 6 servings

2 tablespoons cornmeal
1 (12- to 14-inch) prepared pizza crust, uncooked
3/4 cup prepared tomato or pizza sauce
1 cup sun-dried tomatoes*
1 DOLE® Green Bell Pepper, seeded and chopped
1 can (2 1/4 ounces) sliced ripe olives, drained
1 can (20 ounces) DOLE® Pineapple Tidbits in Juice, drained
1 cup (4 ounces) shredded smoked Gouda cheese
1 cup (4 ounces) shredded fontina cheese
Freshly ground black pepper

• Sprinkle cornmeal on bottom of pizza pan. Place pizza crust on pan. Spread tomato sauce over crust.

• Top with tomatoes, bell pepper, olives and pineapple. Sprinkle with cheeses and pepper.

• Bake in 425°F oven 16 to 20 minutes or until cheese melts and crust browns.

You can purchase sun-dried tomatoes either packed in oil in jars or packaged dry in cellophane. The oil-packed variety tends to be more expensive but are ready to use. The dry variety needs to be poached in liquid before using (see package directions).

Prep time: 20 minutes
Bake time: 20 minutes

HOMEMADE PIZZA

Makes 4 to 6 servings

½ **tablespoon active dry yeast**
1 **teaspoon sugar, divided**
½ **cup warm water
    (105° to 115°F)**
1¾ **cups all-purpose flour, divided**
¾ **teaspoon salt, divided**
2 **tablespoons olive oil, divided**
1 **can (14½ ounces) whole peeled
    tomatoes, undrained**
1 **medium onion, chopped**
1 **clove garlic, minced**
2 **tablespoons tomato paste**
1 **teaspoon dried oregano leaves,
    crushed**
½ **teaspoon dried basil leaves,
    crushed**
⅛ **teaspoon ground black pepper**
1¾ **cups shredded mozzarella
    cheese**
½ **cup freshly grated Parmesan
    cheese**
½ **small red bell pepper, cored
    and seeded**
½ **small green bell pepper, cored
    and seeded**
4 **fresh medium mushrooms**
1 **can (2 ounces) flat anchovy
    fillets, drained (optional)**
⅓ **cup pitted ripe olives, halved**

Sprinkle yeast and ½ teaspoon sugar over ½ cup warm water in small bowl; stir until yeast is dissolved. Let stand 5 minutes or until mixture is bubbly.

Place 1½ cups flour and ¼ teaspoon salt in medium bowl; stir in yeast mixture and 1 tablespoon oil, stirring until smooth, soft dough forms. Place dough on lightly floured surface; flatten slightly. Knead dough using as much of remaining flour as needed to form a stiff, elastic dough.

Shape dough into a ball; place in greased bowl. Turn to grease entire surface. Cover with clean kitchen towel and let dough rise in warm place 30 to 45 minutes or until doubled in bulk. Press two fingertips about ½ inch into dough. Dough is ready if indentations remain after fingers are removed.

For sauce, finely chop tomatoes in can with knife, reserving juice. Heat remaining 1 tablespoon oil in medium saucepan over medium heat. Add onion; cook 5 minutes or until soft. Add garlic; cook 30 seconds more. Add tomatoes and juice, tomato paste, oregano, basil, remaining ½ teaspoon sugar, ½ teaspoon salt and black pepper. Bring to a boil; reduce heat to medium-low. Simmer, uncovered, 10 to 15 minutes or until sauce thickens, stirring occasionally. Pour into bowl; cool.

Punch dough down. Knead briefly on lightly floured surface to distribute air bubbles; let dough rest 5 minutes more. Flatten dough into circle on lightly floured surface. Roll out dough, starting at center and rolling to edges, into 10-inch circle. Place circle in greased 12-inch pizza pan; stretch and pat dough out to edges of pan. Crimp edges to form rim. Cover and let stand 15 minutes.

Preheat oven to 450°F. Mix mozzarella and Parmesan cheeses in small bowl. Cut bell peppers into ¾-inch pieces. Trim mushroom stems; wipe clean with damp kitchen towel and thinly slice. Spread sauce evenly over pizza dough. Sprinkle with ⅔ of cheeses. Arrange bell peppers, mushrooms, anchovies, if desired, and olives over cheese. Sprinkle remaining cheeses on top. Bake 20 minutes or until crust is golden brown. To serve, cut into wedges.

Homemade Pizza

VEGETABLE RICE PIZZA

Makes 4 servings

- 3 cups cooked rice
- 1 egg, beaten
- 1 cup (4 ounces) shredded mozzarella cheese, divided
  Vegetable cooking spray
- 2/3 cup tomato sauce
- 2 teaspoons Italian seasoning
- 1/4 teaspoon garlic powder
- 1/4 teaspoon ground black pepper
- 1 tablespoon grated Parmesan cheese (optional)
- 1 cup (about 4 ounces) sliced fresh mushrooms
- 3/4 cup thinly sliced zucchini
- 1/4 cup sliced ripe olives
- 1/4 cup diced red pepper
- 1 tablespoon snipped parsley

Combine rice, egg and 1/3 cup mozzarella cheese in large bowl. Press into 12-inch pizza pan or 10-inch pie pan coated with cooking spray. Bake at 400°F for 5 minutes. Combine tomato sauce, Italian seasoning, garlic powder and black pepper in small bowl; spread over rice crust. Sprinkle with Parmesan cheese. Layer 1/3 cup mozzarella cheese, mushrooms, zucchini, olives and red pepper. Top with remaining 1/3 cup mozzarella cheese and parsley. Bake at 400°F for 8 to 10 minutes.

PIZZA AUBERGINE

Makes 4 to 6 servings

- 1 small eggplant (about 3/4 pound), halved and thinly sliced
- 1 medium onion, halved and sliced
- 2 tablespoons vegetable oil
- 2 cups sliced mushrooms
- 2 cloves garlic, minced
- 1 (12-inch) prepared, pre-baked pizza crust*
- 1 can (14 1/2 ounces) DEL MONTE® Pizza Style Chunky Tomatoes
- 2 cups shredded mozzarella cheese

Preheat oven to 450°F. In large skillet, cook eggplant and onion in oil over medium-high heat until tender. Add mushrooms and garlic and cook 5 minutes; drain. Place crust on baking sheet. Spread tomatoes evenly over crust. Top with cheese and eggplant mixture. Bake 10 minutes or until hot and bubbly.

Substitute 4 (6-inch) prepared, pre-baked pizza crusts. Refrigerated or frozen pizza dough may also be used; prepare and bake according to package directions.

Prep time: 20 minutes
Cook time: 10 minutes

Vegetable Rice Pizza

FRESH VEGETABLE PIZZA

Makes 1 (10-inch) pizza

1 package (¼ ounce) active dry yeast
1 teaspoon sugar
½ cup warm water (120° to 130°F)
3 large cloves fresh garlic, divided
1¾ cups sifted all-purpose flour, divided
1 tablespoon oil
1 teaspoon salt, divided
3 small firm, ripe tomatoes
1 cup thinly sliced zucchini
1 cup sliced fresh mushrooms
¼ cup sliced green onions
1½ cups (6 ounces) shredded Monterey Jack cheese, divided
½ teaspoon dried basil leaves, crushed
½ teaspoon Italian seasoning
2 tablespoons grated Parmesan cheese

Sprinkle yeast and sugar over warm water in large bowl; let stand 5 minutes to soften. Peel and press through garlic press 1 clove garlic into yeast mixture. Add ¾ cup flour. Beat with electric mixer until smooth. Stir in oil and ½ teaspoon salt. Gradually stir in remaining 1 cup flour to make a moderately stiff dough. Turn out onto floured surface and knead about 2 minutes or until smooth. Place in greased 10-inch pizza pan and press out to cover pan; set aside.

Blanch tomatoes by dropping into boiling water to cover. Let stand 10 seconds. Lift out and peel off skins. Remove cores and cut tomatoes into slices about ⅜ inch thick to measure about 2 cups. Drop zucchini slices into boiling water and cook 1 minute. Drain well. Combine with mushrooms and onions in large bowl. Press remaining 2 cloves peeled garlic over vegetable mixture; mix well. Sprinkle 1 cup Monterey Jack cheese over dough. Spoon ½ of vegetable mixture over cheese. Arrange tomato slices on top, overlapping if necessary. Top with remaining vegetable mixture. Sprinkle with basil, Italian seasoning, remaining ½ teaspoon salt, remaining ½ cup Monterey Jack cheese and Parmesan cheese. Preheat oven to 375°F. Let pizza stand 15 minutes or until edges of dough feel light to touch. Bake 40 minutes or until crust is golden brown.

Favorite recipe from **Fresh Garlic Association**

CHEESY ASPARAGUS PIZZA

Makes 4 to 6 servings

½ cup mayonnaise
2 tablespoons grated Parmesan cheese
¼ teaspoon dry mustard
2 egg whites
1 (12-inch) BOBOLI® Brand Italian Bread Shell *or* 4 small 6-inch bread shells
6 medium asparagus spears, cooked and cut into 1-inch pieces

Blend together mayonnaise, cheese and mustard. Beat egg whites until stiff peaks form; fold into mayonnaise mixture. Spoon mixture on Boboli® Italian bread shell. Arrange cut asparagus over mayonnaise mixture. Bake on ungreased baking sheet at 450°F about 8 to 10 minutes or until puffed and lightly browned.

VEGETABLE PIZZA

Makes 4 servings
(2 wedges per serving)

1 small zucchini, sliced
(about 1 cup)
1 medium onion, cut into eighths
1 small green bell pepper, cut
into thin strips
2 cloves garlic, minced
¹⁄₂ teaspoon dried oregano leaves,
crushed
¹⁄₂ teaspoon dried basil leaves,
crushed
¹⁄₈ teaspoon pepper
2 tablespoons olive or
vegetable oil
³⁄₄ cup HEINZ® Chili Sauce
¹⁄₄ cup grated Parmesan cheese
1 pre-baked pizza shell (12-inch)
1¹⁄₂ cups shredded mozzarella
cheese

In 2-quart saucepan, sauté zucchini, onion, green pepper, garlic, oregano, basil and pepper in oil until vegetables are tender-crisp. Stir in chili sauce and Parmesan cheese; simmer 5 minutes, stirring occasionally. Place pizza shell on baking sheet. Spoon vegetable mixture evenly over pizza shell; sprinkle mozzarella cheese on top. Bake in preheated 425°F oven, 10 to 12 minutes or until shell is lightly browned. Cut pizza into 8 wedges.

MARINATED BELL PEPPER & MUSHROOM PIZZA

Makes 1 (12-inch) deep-dish pizza

Marinated Mushrooms
(recipe follows)
Marinated Bell Peppers
(recipe follows)
6 to 8 eggplant slices, unpeeled
Olive oil
Herb Mixture (recipe follows)
6 plum tomatoes
1 pound (1 loaf) frozen bread
dough, thawed
³⁄₄ cup (6 ounces) shredded
Wisconsin Whole Milk
Mozzarella cheese
1 cup (4 ounces) shredded
Wisconsin Provolone cheese

Prepare Marinated Mushrooms; set aside. Prepare Marinated Bell Peppers; set aside.

Place eggplant in colander over sink; rinse slices well. Salt slices; drain 1 hour. Preheat oven to 425°F. Rinse salt from eggplant; pat dry with paper towels. Lay slices on baking sheet and brush with olive oil. Bake, turning once, ¹⁄₂ hour or until slightly softened. Prepare Herb Mixture. Blanch tomatoes 1 minute in boiling water; peel, seed and crush. Combine tomato mixture and Herb Mixture.

Increase oven temperature to 475°F. Roll bread dough into 14-inch circle. Press onto bottom and up sides of 12-inch deep-dish pizza pan. Layer toppings in the following order: tomato-herb mixture, eggplant slices, drained Marinated Bell Peppers, drained Marinated Mushrooms and cheeses. Bake on lower rack in oven 10 to 12 minutes or until crust is golden brown.

Marinated Bell Pepper & Mushroom Pizza

Marinated Mushrooms

4 ounces fresh mushrooms
1 tablespoon butter
1 cup olive oil
1 bay leaf
   Freshly ground black pepper to taste
1 tablespoon chopped parsley
   Dash *each* dried thyme leaves and dried marjoram leaves, crushed

Wash and quarter mushrooms. Melt butter over medium heat in medium skillet until melted and bubbly. Add mushrooms; cook and stir until browned. Cool. Combine remaining ingredients in large jar with lid; cover and shake to combine. Add cooled mushrooms and marinate at least 1 hour.

Marinated Bell Peppers

1 cup olive oil
1 garlic clove, minced
2 tablespoons balsamic vinegar
1 tablespoon red wine vinegar
1/2 teaspoon salt
   Freshly ground black pepper to taste
3 ounces green bell peppers, cut into strips

Combine all ingredients except green pepper strips in large jar with lid; cover and shake to combine. Add green pepper strips and marinate at least 1 hour.

Herb Mixture: Combine 1 tablespoon torn fresh basil leaves, 1 minced garlic clove, dash *each* dried marjoram leaves, rubbed sage leaves and sugar, and salt and pepper to taste in small bowl; blend well.

Favorite recipe from **Wisconsin Milk Marketing Board © 1993**

ANTIPASTO MINI PIZZAS

Makes 8 servings

1³/₄ cups (14.5-ounce can)
    CONTADINA® Pasta Ready
    Tomatoes
³/₄ cup (4-ounce can) water-
    packed artichoke hearts,
    drained and coarsely
    chopped
¹/₂ cup chopped green bell pepper
¹/₂ cup (2-ounce can) sliced ripe
    olives, drained
2 tablespoons grated Parmesan
    cheese
8 plain bagels, sliced horizontally
    and lightly toasted
1 cup (4 ounces) grated
    mozzarella cheese

In medium bowl, combine tomatoes, artichoke hearts, bell pepper, olives and Parmesan cheese. Spoon about 2¹/₂ tablespoons sauce and vegetable mixture onto each bagel half. Sprinkle mozzarella cheese evenly over top. Bake in preheated 400°F. oven for 6 to 8 minutes or until heated through.

Hint: For appetizer servings, cut sliced bagels in half and proceed as above.

ROMA TOMATO PIZZAS

Makes 2 (15-inch) pizzas

2 loaves (2 pounds) frozen bread
    dough, thawed
¹/₃ cup olive oil
2 cups (2 medium) thinly sliced
    onions
2 garlic cloves, minced
12 Roma (Italian plum) tomatoes,
    sliced ¹/₈ inch thick
1 teaspoon dried basil leaves,
    crushed
1 teaspoon dried oregano leaves,
    crushed
    Freshly ground black pepper
¹/₂ cup grated Parmesan cheese
1 can (2¹/₄ ounces) sliced, pitted
    ripe olives, drained
    Green and yellow bell pepper
    strips

Preheat oven to 450°F. Roll out each loaf on lightly floured surface into 15-inch circle; press each into greased 15-inch pizza pan or stretch into 15×10-inch baking pan. Crimp edges to form rim; prick several times with fork. Bake crusts 10 minutes. Remove from oven; set aside.

Reduce oven temperature to 400°F. Heat oil in large skillet over medium-high heat until hot. Add onions and garlic; cook and stir 6 to 8 minutes or until onions are tender. Divide onion mixture (including olive oil) between crusts. Arrange tomato slices evenly over onion mixture. Sprinkle each pizza with ¹/₂ teaspoon basil leaves, ¹/₂ teaspoon oregano and black pepper to taste. Sprinkle each pizza with ¹/₄ cup Parmesan cheese. Top with olives and desired amount of bell peppers. Bake 10 to 15 minutes or until toppings are heated through.

Roma Tomato Pizza

DAIRYLAND COUNTRY OAT PIZZA

Makes 4 small pizzas

2½ to 3 cups all-purpose flour, divided
1 package (¼ ounce) fast-rising dry yeast
1½ teaspoons salt
1 cup very warm water (120° to 130°F)
6 tablespoons vegetable oil, divided
1 cup rolled oats
2 cups sliced onions
2 large bell peppers (red and/or yellow), seeded and cut into thin strips
2 cloves garlic, minced
Salt and pepper to taste
2 tablespoons chopped fresh basil leaves *or* 2 teaspoons dried basil leaves, crushed
2 cups (8 ounces) shredded Wisconsin Medium Cheddar cheese, divided

Combine 1½ cups flour, yeast, salt, water and 3 tablespoons oil in large mixing bowl. Beat at low speed 1 minute; beat at medium speed 3 minutes. Mix in oats and enough of remaining flour to make a firm dough. Knead on floured surface 3 minutes. Divide dough into 4 equal portions. Pat and roll each into a 6- to 7-inch circle. Place on 2 baking sheets. Cover with clean kitchen towels; set aside in warm place 20 minutes.

Preheat oven to 425°F. Heat remaining 3 tablespoons oil in large skillet over medium heat until hot. Add onions; cook and stir 5 minutes. Add bell peppers and garlic; cook and stir 10 to 15 minutes or until onions are transparent and peppers are limp. Mix in salt, pepper and

basil. Sprinkle ¼ cup Cheddar cheese on each pizza crust. Top with onion mixture, dividing equally and spreading to within ½ inch of edges. Sprinkle remaining 1 cup cheese evenly over onion mixture. Bake 20 minutes or until crust is crisp and lightly browned.

Favorite recipe from **Wisconsin Milk Marketing Board © 1993**

VEGETABLE GARDEN PIZZA

Makes 4 to 6 servings

1 (12-inch) prepared, pre-baked pizza crust*
1 can (14½ ounces) DEL MONTE® Pizza Style Chunky Tomatoes
2 cups shredded mozzarella cheese
1 small zucchini, thinly sliced
1 cup sliced mushrooms
¼ cup sliced green onions
2 tablespoons grated Parmesan cheese
¼ teaspoon dried thyme, crushed

Preheat oven to 450°F. Place pizza crust on baking sheet. Spread tomatoes evenly over crust. Top with mozzarella cheese, zucchini, mushrooms and green onions. Sprinkle with Parmesan cheese and thyme. Bake 10 minutes or until hot and bubbly.

Substitute 4 (6-inch) prepared, pre-baked pizza crusts. Refrigerated or frozen pizza dough may also be used; prepare and bake according to package directions.

Prep time: 15 minutes
Cook time: 10 minutes

HARVEST PIZZA

Makes about 4 servings

**4 tablespoons WISH-BONE®
    Classic Olive Oil Italian
    Dressing, divided**
**2 cups Suggested Fresh
    Vegetables***
**1 pound fresh or thawed frozen
    pizza or bread dough**
**1 cup shredded mozzarella
    cheese (4 ounces)**
**2 tablespoons grated Parmesan
    cheese**

In medium skillet, heat 2
tablespoons classic olive oil Italian
dressing and cook Suggested Fresh
Vegetables over medium heat,
stirring occasionally, 3 minutes or
until crisp-tender; set aside.

Preheat oven to 450°F. Divide
dough and shape into 2 balls. Into
lightly oiled pizza pans or cookie
sheets, press dough to form desired
shapes. Brush each crust with 1
tablespoon classic olive oil Italian
dressing; set aside.

With slotted spoon, top each crust
with 1/2 of the cooked vegetables and
cheeses. Bake 18 minutes or until
crusts are golden brown. Sprinkle, if
desired, with sliced fresh basil or
green onions and freshly ground
black pepper.

***Suggested Fresh Vegetables:** Use
any combination of the following:
sliced zucchini, yellow squash,
tomatoes, eggplant, mushrooms,
green beans; red, yellow or green
bell pepper strips; asparagus cut into
2-inch pieces; snow peas.

Note: Also terrific with Wish-Bone®
Italian, Robusto Italian or Lite Italian
Dressing.

Harvest Pizza

MUSHROOM PIZZA

Makes 1 serving

**   Vegetable cooking spray**
1/2 cup sliced mushrooms
**3 tablespoons diced green bell
    pepper**
3 tablespoons fresh diced tomato
1 garlic clove, minced
**1 tablespoon chopped parsley
    Salt and black pepper to taste**
1 (6-inch) pita bread
**1 ounce Jarlsberg or Jarlsberg Lite
    cheese, shredded**

Preheat oven to 350°F. Coat medium
skillet with vegetable spray; heat
over medium heat until hot. Add
mushrooms, green pepper, tomato
and garlic; cook and stir until
vegetables are soft. Add parsley, salt
and black pepper. Evenly distribute
mushroom mixture on top of pita
bread. Sprinkle with cheese. Put
pizza on baking sheet; bake 20
minutes or until cheese is melted.

Favorite recipe from **Norseland Foods, Inc.**

SWEET PIZZA PIES

Indulge in brownie and cookie crusts covered with candy and fruit! Pizza can be more than a snack or main course. Make Banana Split Dessert Pizza or Chocolate Lovers' Brownie Pizza the grand finale.

BANANA BERRY BROWNIE PIZZA

Makes 10 to 12 servings

⅓ **cup cold water**
1 **(15 oz.) pkg. brownie mix**
¼ **cup oil**
1 **egg**
1 **(8 oz.) pkg. PHILADELPHIA BRAND® Cream Cheese, softened**
¼ **cup sugar**
1 **egg**
1 **teaspoon vanilla**
  Strawberry slices
  Banana slices
2 **(1 oz.) squares BAKER'S® Semi-Sweet Chocolate, melted**

• Preheat oven to 350°F.

• Bring water to boil.

• Mix together brownie mix, water, oil and egg in large bowl until well blended.

• Pour into greased and floured 12-inch pizza pan.

• Bake 25 minutes.

• Beat cream cheese, sugar, remaining egg and vanilla in small mixing bowl at medium speed with electric mixer until well blended. Pour over crust.

• Continue baking 15 minutes. Cool. Top with fruit; drizzle with chocolate. Garnish with mint leaves, if desired.

Prep time: 35 minutes
Cooking time: 40 minutes

Microwave Tip: To melt chocolate, place unwrapped chocolate squares in small bowl. Microwave on HIGH 1 to 2 minutes or until almost melted. Stir until chocolate is completely melted.

Banana Berry Brownie Pizza

FRESH FRUIT PIZZA COOKIE

Makes 8 servings

1 package (20 ounces)
   refrigerated chocolate chip
   cookie dough
1 package (8 ounces) light cream
   cheese
¹/₃ cup sugar
1 teaspoon vanilla extract
1 DOLE® Fresh Pineapple
2 DOLE® Kiwifruit, peeled and
   sliced
1 DOLE® Banana, peeled and
   sliced
¹/₄ cup raspberries (optional)
¹/₄ cup apricot jam, melted

• Press small pieces of cookie dough into 14-inch pizza pan. Bake in 350°F oven 12 to 15 minutes or until browned and puffed. Cool completely in pan on wire rack.

• Beat cream cheese, sugar and vanilla in medium bowl until blended. Spread over cooled cookie.

• Twist crown from pineapple. Cut pineapple in half lengthwise. Refrigerate one-half for another use, such as fruit salad. Cut fruit from remaining half into thin wedges.

• Arrange pineapple around outer edge of cream cheese. Arrange kiwifruit, banana slices and raspberries in flower pattern over pineapple. Brush with jam.

Prep time: 20 minutes
Bake time: 15 minutes

Fresh Fruit Pizza Cookie

PINEAPPLE CREAM CHEESE PIZZA

Makes 16 servings

1 loaf (1 pound) frozen bread
   dough, thawed and cut in half
2 packages (8 ounces each)
   cream cheese, softened
¹/₂ cup sugar
6 tablespoons flour
2 egg yolks
   Grated peel and juice from
   1 DOLE® Lemon
2 cans (8¹/₄ ounces each) DOLE®
   Crushed Pineapple in Syrup,*
   drained
²/₃ cup strawberry jam
2 tablespoons DOLE® Sliced
   Almonds, toasted

Use pineapple packed in juice, if desired.

• Press dough into 2 greased 12-inch pizza pans.

• Beat cream cheese, sugar, flour, egg yolks, 1 teaspoon lemon peel and 2 teaspoons lemon juice until smooth. Stir in pineapple. Spread mixture evenly over pizzas to within 1/2 inch of edges.

• Bake in 400°F oven 15 minutes or until browned.

• Spread each with jam and sprinkle with almonds. Bake 5 minutes longer.

Prep time: 20 minutes
Bake time: 20 minutes

CHOCOLATE PIZZA

Makes 10 to 12 servings

1 package (12 ounces) BAKER'S® Semi-Sweet Real Chocolate Chips
1 pound white almond bark, divided
2 cups KRAFT® Miniature Marshmallows
1 cup crisp rice cereal
1 cup peanuts
1 jar (6 ounces) red maraschino cherries, drained, halved
3 tablespoons green maraschino cherries, drained, quartered
1/3 cup BAKER'S® ANGEL FLAKE® Coconut
1 teaspoon oil

• Microwave chips and 14 ounces of the almond bark in 2-quart microwave-safe bowl on HIGH 2 minutes; stir. Continue microwaving 1 to 2 minutes or until smooth when stirred, stirring every 30 seconds.

• Stir in marshmallows, cereal and peanuts. Pour onto greased 12-inch pizza pan. Top with cherries; sprinkle with coconut.

• Microwave remaining 2 ounces almond bark and oil in 1-cup glass measuring cup 1 minute; stir. Continue microwaving 30 seconds to 1 minute or until smooth when stirred, stirring every 15 seconds. Drizzle over coconut.

• Refrigerate until firm. Store at room temperature.

Gift Giving Tip: For smaller pizzas, spoon chocolate mixture onto greased cookie sheet, forming 3 (7-inch) or 4 (6-inch) circles with back of wooden spoon. Continue as directed. Place on tray or cardboard circle, wrap in colored cellophane paper or plastic wrap and tie with colorful bow.

Prep time: 15 minutes plus refrigerating
Microwave cooking time: 6 minutes

Chocolate Pizza

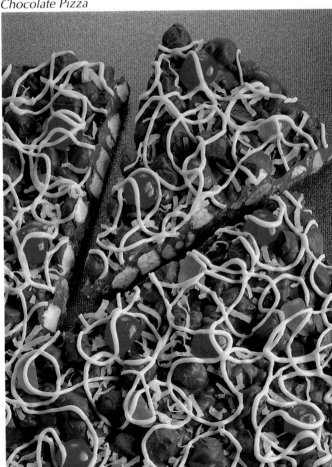

BROWNIE PIZZA

Makes 12 servings

BROWNIE LAYER:
- 4 squares BAKER'S® Unsweetened Chocolate
- ¾ cup (1½ sticks) margarine or butter
- 2 cups sugar
- 4 eggs
- 1 teaspoon vanilla
- 1 cup all-purpose flour

TOPPING:
- 1 package (8 ounces) PHILADELPHIA BRAND® Cream Cheese, softened
- ¼ cup sugar
- 1 egg
- ½ teaspoon vanilla
  Assorted sliced fruit
- 2 squares BAKER'S® Semi-Sweet Chocolate

HEAT oven to 350°F. Line 12×½-inch pizza pan with foil (to lift brownie from pan after baking); grease foil.

MICROWAVE unsweetened chocolate and margarine in large microwavable bowl on HIGH 2 minutes or until margarine is melted. **Stir until chocolate is completely melted.**

STIR 2 cups sugar into melted chocolate mixture. Mix in 4 eggs and 1 teaspoon vanilla until well blended. Stir in flour. Spread in prepared pan. Bake for 30 minutes.

MIX cream cheese, ¼ cup sugar, 1 egg and ½ teaspoon vanilla in same bowl until well blended. Pour over baked brownie crust.

BAKE 10 minutes longer or until toothpick inserted into center comes out with fudgy crumbs. **Do not overbake.** Cool in pan. Lift brownie pizza out of pan; peel off foil. Place brownie pizza on serving plate. Arrange fruit over cream cheese layer. Drizzle with melted semi-sweet chocolate.

Prep time: 30 minutes
Baking time: 40 minutes

Brownie Pizza

PEANUT APPLE DESSERT PIZZA

Makes 6 to 8 servings

- 1 box pie crust mix (for 9-inch pie), divided
- ½ cup sugar
- ½ cup finely chopped salted peanuts
- 1 teaspoon ground cinnamon
- ¼ teaspoon ground nutmeg
- ¼ cup peanut butter
- 3 to 4 medium apples, peeled and sliced into ½-inch-thick wedges

Make ½ of pie crust mix as package directs. Cut 12-inch circle from aluminum foil. Roll pastry on foil to fit circle. Trim off edge. Put foil and pastry onto baking sheet. Combine remaining pie crust mix, sugar, peanuts, cinnamon and nutmeg. Cut in peanut butter with pastry blender or 2 knives to make fine crumbs. Beginning 1 inch from outside edge, arrange apple slices, overlapping slightly, in circle on pastry. Arrange another circle of apple slices inside this circle. If necessary, arrange remaining apple slices in center of pastry. Sprinkle with crumb mixture. Turn up edge of foil *with* pastry. Flute pastry edge. Bake in 450°F oven for 20 to 25 minutes or until crust is browned and apples are tender. Cut into wedges. Serve warm.

Favorite recipe from **Oklahoma Peanut Commission**

Nestlé® Candy Shop Pizza

NESTLÉ® CANDY SHOP PIZZA

Makes about 12 servings

1½ **cups all-purpose flour**
 ½ **teaspoon baking soda**
 ½ **teaspoon salt**
10 **tablespoons (1¼ sticks) butter, softened**
 ½ **cup granulated sugar**
 ½ **cup firmly packed brown sugar**
 1 **egg**
 ½ **teaspoon vanilla extract**
 2 **cups (12-oz. pkg.) NESTLÉ® Toll House® Semi-Sweet Chocolate Morsels, divided**
 ½ **cup peanut butter**
 1 **cup chopped candy such as NESTLÉ® Crunch® bars, Alpine White® bars, Butterfinger® bars, Baby Ruth® bars, Goobers® and Raisinets®**

Preheat oven to 375°F. Lightly grease 12- to 14-inch pizza pan *or* 15½×10½×1-inch baking pan. In small bowl, combine flour, baking soda and salt; set aside.

In large mixer bowl, beat butter, granulated sugar and brown sugar until creamy. Beat in egg and vanilla extract. Gradually beat in flour mixture. Stir in 1 cup semi-sweet chocolate morsels. Spread in prepared pan. Bake 20 to 24 minutes until lightly browned.

Immediately sprinkle remaining 1 cup semi-sweet chocolate morsels over crust; drop peanut butter by spoonfuls on morsels. Let stand 5 minutes or until morsels become soft and shiny. Gently spread chocolate and peanut butter evenly over crust. Decorate pizza with candy. Cut into wedges; serve warm.

CHOCOLATE LOVERS' BROWNIE PIZZA

Makes 12 servings

1 package DUNCAN HINES®
   Chocolate Lovers' Milk
   Chocolate Chunk
   Brownie Mix
1 egg
1/3 cup CRISCO® Oil or
   CRISCO® PURITAN® Oil
2 tablespoons water
   Strawberry slices
   Kiwifruit wedges
   Pineapple pieces
   Vanilla ice cream
   Chocolate syrup

1. Preheat oven to 350°F. Grease 13-inch round pizza pan.

2. Combine brownie mix, egg, oil and water in large bowl. Stir with spoon until well blended, about 50 strokes. Spread in pan. Bake at 350°F for 18 to 20 minutes. Cool completely.

3. Cut into wedges; decorate with assorted fruit. Top with scoops of ice cream, then drizzle with chocolate syrup.

Tip: For convenience, purchase pre-cut fruit from the salad bar at your local grocery store.

FRUIT AND COOKIE PIZZA

Makes 8 servings

1 package (20 ounces)
   refrigerated chocolate chip
   cookie dough
1 can (20 ounces) DOLE®
   Pineapple Slices in Syrup*
1 package (8 ounces) light cream
   cheese, softened
1/3 cup sugar
1 teaspoon vanilla extract
1 DOLE® Banana, peeled and
   sliced
1 DOLE® Kiwifruit, peeled and
   sliced
1/4 cup DOLE® Strawberries
1/3 cup DOLE® Raspberries
1/4 cup bottled chocolate sauce

• Press small pieces of cookie dough into 14-inch pizza pan. Bake in 350°F oven until browned and puffed. Cool completely in pan on wire rack.

• Drain pineapple; reserve 2 tablespoons syrup.

• Beat cream cheese, sugar, reserved syrup and vanilla in medium bowl until smooth. Spread over cooled cookie.

• Arrange pineapple slices over outer edge of cream cheese. Arrange bananas, kiwifruit and strawberries in flower pattern over pineapple. Arrange raspberries in center of pineapple slices.

• Spoon chocolate sauce over fruit.

Use pineapple packed in juice, if desired.

Prep time: 15 minutes
Bake time: 12 minutes

Chocolate Lovers' Brownie Pizza

Brownie Pudding Pizza

BROWNIE PUDDING PIZZA

Makes 8 servings

1 package (10½ ounces)
  microwave brownie mix (plus
  ingredients to prepare mix)
1¼ cups cold milk
1 package (4-serving size) JELL-O®
  Instant Pudding, any flavor
1 cup thawed COOL WHIP®
  Whipped Topping
2 cups cut-up fruit

PREPARE brownie mix in medium
bowl, following package directions.
Pour mixture into 9-inch
microwavable pie plate. Microwave,
following package directions for 9-
inch square pan. (Plate will be hot.)
Cool.

POUR cold milk into small bowl.
Add pudding mix. Beat with wire
whisk until well blended, about
2 minutes. Let pudding stand 5
minutes.

STIR whipped topping into pudding
very gently until mixture is all the
same color. If you do not want to
prepare and eat pizza right away,
put pudding mixture into refrigerator
to chill until serving time. Just before
serving, spoon pudding mixture over
brownies, spreading with back of
spoon to cover evenly.

CUT into wedges. Top each wedge
with fruit, arranging in whatever
design you like.

BANANA SPLIT DESSERT PIZZA

Makes one 12-inch pizza

1 (14-ounce) can EAGLE® Brand
  Sweetened Condensed Milk
  (NOT evaporated milk)
½ cup BORDEN® or MEADOW
  GOLD® Sour Cream
6 tablespoons REALEMON®
  Lemon Juice from
  Concentrate
1 teaspoon vanilla extract
½ cup plus 1 tablespoon
  margarine or butter, softened
¼ cup firmly packed brown sugar
1 cup unsifted flour
¼ cup quick-cooking oats
¼ cup finely chopped nuts
3 medium bananas
1 (8-ounce) can sliced pineapple,
  drained and cut in half
  Maraschino cherries and nuts
1 (1-ounce) square semi-sweet
  chocolate

Preheat oven to 375°F. In medium
bowl, combine sweetened
condensed milk, sour cream, *¼ cup*
ReaLemon® brand and vanilla; mix
well. Chill. In large mixer bowl, beat
½ cup margarine and sugar until
fluffy; add flour, oats and nuts. Mix
well. On lightly greased pizza pan or

baking sheet, press dough into 12-inch circle, forming rim around edge. Prick with fork. Bake 10 to 12 minutes or until golden brown. Cool. Slice bananas; arrange *2 bananas* on cooled crust. Spoon filling evenly over bananas. Dip remaining banana slices in remaining *2 tablespoons* ReaLemon® brand; drain and arrange on top along with pineapple, cherries and additional nuts. In small saucepan, over low heat, melt chocolate with remaining *1 tablespoon* margarine; drizzle over pie. Chill thoroughly. Refrigerate leftovers.

Tip: Crust and filling can be made in advance. Store crust at room temperature; refrigerate filling.

COOKIE PIZZA

Makes about 8 servings

1 package (20 ounces) refrigerated sugar cookie dough
1 package (5.4 ounces) bite-size chewy real fruit snacks
   Decorating icing, colored sugar crystals or other cake decorations (optional)

Preheat oven to 350°F. In 12- or 14-inch pizza pan lined with aluminum foil and sprayed with non-stick cooking spray, press cookie dough. Press fruit snacks into pizza in decorative designs. Bake 20 minutes or until cookie edges are golden brown. On wire rack, cool 10 minutes; loosen from pan and remove foil. Decorate with icing.

Favorite recipe from **The Lipton Kitchens**

GELATIN PIZZA

Makes 10 to 12 servings

4 packages (4-serving size each) *or* 2 packages (8-serving size each) JELL-O® Gelatin, any flavor
2½ cups boiling water
   No-stick cooking spray
1 cup thawed COOL WHIP® Whipped Topping
2 cups cut-up fruit

POUR gelatin into bowl. Add 2½ cups boiling water to gelatin. Stir until gelatin is completely dissolved, about 2 minutes. Spray pizza pan with no-stick cooking spray. Pour gelatin mixture into pizza pan. Put pan into refrigerator to chill until firm, about 3 hours.

TAKE pan out of refrigerator when ready to serve. Put about 1 inch of warm water in sink. Carefully dip just bottom of pan into warm water for 15 seconds. Spread whipped topping over gelatin just before serving, leaving about 1 inch of space around outside edge of gelatin for pizza "crust."

TOP pizza with fruit, arranging fruit in whatever design you like. Cut pizza into wedges.

Gelatin Pizza

ACKNOWLEDGMENTS

The publishers would like to thank the companies and organizations listed below for the use of their recipes in this publication.

Best Foods, a Division of CPC International Inc.
Bongrain Cheese U.S.A.
Borden Kitchens, Borden, Inc.
California Olive Industry
California Poultry Industry Federation
Canned Food Information Council
Checkerboard Kitchens, Ralston Purina Company
Contadina Foods, Inc., Nestlé Food Company
Del Monte Foods
Dole Food Company, Inc.
The Fresh Garlic Association
Heinz U.S.A.
The HVR Company
Idaho Bean Commission
Kellogg Company
Kikkoman International Inc.

Kraft General Foods, Inc.
Lawry's® Foods, Inc.
Thomas J. Lipton Co.
McIlhenny Company
National Fisheries Institute
National Live Stock and Meat Board
Nestlé Food Company
Norseland Foods, Inc.
Oklahoma Peanut Commission
Pace Foods, Inc.
The Procter & Gamble Company, Inc.
The Quaker Oats Company
Reckitt & Colman, Inc.
Sargento Cheese Company, Inc.
StarKist Seafood Company
Tholstrup Cheese U.S.A., Inc.
Uncle Ben's Rice
USA Rice Council
Wisconsin Milk Marketing Board

PHOTO CREDITS

The publishers would like to thank the companies and organizations listed below for the use of their photographs in this publication.

Borden Kitchens, Borden, Inc.
California Poultry Industry Federation
Canned Food Information Council
Contadina Foods, Inc., Nestlé Food Company
Del Monte Foods
Dole Food Company, Inc.
The Fresh Garlic Association
Kikkoman International Inc.
Kraft General Foods, Inc.
Lawry's® Foods, Inc.
Thomas J. Lipton Co.

McIlhenny Company
National Fisheries Institute
National Live Stock and Meat Board
Nestlé Food Company
Oklahoma Peanut Commission
Pace Foods, Inc.
The Procter & Gamble Company, Inc.
StarKist Seafood Company
Tholstrup Cheese U.S.A., Inc.
Uncle Ben's Rice
USA Rice Council
Wisconsin Milk Marketing Board

INDEX